# Slice of The Wild
## Cut and cook game for your table

*Hope the freezer's full!*

Eileen Clarke

www.riflesandrecipes.com

Copyright © 2009 by Eileen Clarke
Words & photos copyright © 2009 by Eileen Clarke
All rights reserved, including the right of reproduction in whole or in part in any form, electronic or mechanical, including photocopying, recording, or by any information storage and retrieval system, in use now or invented after publication, without the written permission of the author.

All requests should be addressed to:
Deep Creek Press
P.O. Box 579
Townsend, MT 59644

Edited by John Barsness ~ Designed by Eileen Clarke

Published and Distributed by:
Deep Creek Press
P.O. Box 579
Townsend, MT 59644
www.riflesandrecipes.com

Printed in the United States of America

ISBN: 978-0-9822072-0-8

Published March 2009

# Table of Contents

Introduction: No More Mystery Meat    11

Top Ten Tips For Trophy Eats    12

## Field To Gambrel

The Devil Is In The Details    20
How Do They Taste?    22
Rogues' Gallery    24
Photos: Dressing, Cooling, Skinning, Aging    32
Moving Day    40

## Gambrel To Table

The Basic Tools for Butchering    44
The Choices: Parting It Out    45
T&T Test: Real World Taste Test    46
Five Easy Pieces: Four Quarters And Tenders    47
Custom Cutting For Your Table    52
How Much Do You Get?    58

# The Tender End: Steaks and Medallions

| | |
|---|---|
| Grilled Venison Steaks with Garlic Butter | 60 |
| Tips & Tactics: Steaks from Tenders | 60 |
| Grilled Venison Steaks with Herbed Butter | 61 |
| Wild Sides: More Herbed Butters | 61 |
| Dr. Pepper's Marinated Steaks | 62 |
| Wild Sides: Grilled Chiles Rellenos | 62 |
| The Four Ingredient Wonder | 63 |
| Wild Sides: Grilled Sweet Bells | 63 |
| Tips & Tactics: Re-Using Marinades | 63 |
| Chop Chop Salad Dressing Marinade | 64 |
| Zesty Dijon Salad Dressing Marinade | 64 |
| Grilled Steaks with Chipotle Cream Sauce | 65 |
| Gideon's Grub Rub Steaks | 66 |
| Wild Sides: Grilled Corn on the Cob | 66 |
| Balsamic Parmesan Marinated Steaks | 67 |
| Tips & Tactics: What the Marinade Helps | 67 |
| Pomegranate Balsamic Vinegar Marinated Steaks | 68 |
| Wild Sides: Grilled Cherry Tomatoes | 68 |
| Bacon-Wrapped Medallions | 69 |
| Wild Sides: Savory Pasta | 69 |
| Tips & Tactics: Grilling Temperature | 69 |
| Hot & Sweet Venison Kabobs | 70 |
| Wild Sides: Doctor E-Z Beans | 70 |
| Tips & Tactics: Is Wood Better? | 70 |

| | |
|---|---|
| Chili-On-A-Stick | 71 |
| Wild Sides: Tex-Mex Potato Salad | 71 |
| Old World Marinated Venison & Potato Kabobs | 72 |
| Red Wine Marinated Venison Kabobs | 73 |
| Wild Sides: Four Bean Salad | 73 |
| | |
| Blood Orange Marinated Venison Kabobs | 74 |
| Tips & Tactics: When Is It Done? | 74 |
| Kabobs with Tangy Peanut Marinade and Dipping Sauce | 75 |
| Wild Sides: What Goes With? | 75 |
| Tasty Quesadillas | 76 |
| | |
| Wild Sides: Fresh Salsa | 76 |
| Ten Minute Steaks with Herbed Madeira Sauce | 77 |
| Tips & Tactics: Cooking With Spirits | 77 |
| Quick Italian Tender Chunks | 78 |
| Wild Sides: Sautéed Pepper and Onions | 78 |
| | |
| Asian-American Stir-Fry | 79 |
| Very-Asian Stir-Fry | 80 |
| Pan-Roasted Steaks in Citrus Marinade | 81 |
| Tips & Tactics: Cooking Temperature | 81 |
| Pan-Roasted Steaks with Mushroom Sauce | 82 |
| | |
| Wild Sides: Super Creamy Mac & Cheese | 82 |
| Pan-Roasted Steaks in Creamy Garlic Sauce | 83 |
| Tips & Tactics: A Perfect Finish | 83 |
| Pan-Roasted Safari Steaks | 84 |
| Wild Sides: Oven Fried Potatoes | 84 |

# The Tender End: Hind Quarters and Tenderloins

| | |
|---|---|
| Dry Roasting Made Easy and Predictable | 98 |
| My Dry Roasting Table | 101 |
| Your Dry Roasting Table | 102 |
| The $5 Solution | 103 |
| | |
| Indirect al Fresco Roast | 104 |
| Wild Sides: Red Ranch Rotini Salad | 104 |
| Grilled Tenderloin Stuffed with Piggy Salsa | 105 |
| Wild Sides: Sweet and Sour Slaw | 105 |
| Pancetta Rump | 106 |
| | |
| Wild Sides: Irish Mashed Potatoes | 106 |
| Traditional (Well, Sorta) Venison Wellington | 107 |
| Wild Sides: Shiitake-Laced Scalloped Potatoes | 108 |
| Easy Pesto Wellington | 109 |
| Wild Sides: Roasted Veggies | 109 |
| | |
| Spike: The Larded Roast | 110 |
| Wild Sides: Half-Mashed Potatoes | 110 |
| Succulent Roast Tenderloin | 111 |
| Wild Sides: Savory Rice | 111 |
| Gideon's Grub Rub Goes A-Roasting | 112 |

# The Middle: Ribs, Briskets, and Flank Steaks

| | |
|---|---|
| Tasty and Tender Oven Bag Flank Steaks | 114 |
| Wild Sides: Kool, Keen, Quinoa Salad | 114 |
| Flank Steak Fajitas | 115 |
| Christmas Chorizo Rollups | 116 |
| | |
| Bloody Mary Brisket | 117 |
| Wild Sides: Chipotle Slaw | 117 |
| Dry Rub Brisket | 118 |
| Sweet and Zingy Brisket | 119 |
| Wild Sides: Chilled Broccoli Salad | 119 |
| | |
| Corned Brisket | 120 |
| Carolina-Style Brisket | 121 |
| Wild Sides: Two-Can Baked Beans | 121 |
| Tipsy Brisket | 122 |
| Cheatin' Ribs | 123 |
| | |
| Tips & Tactics: Better Ribs | 123 |
| Brisket in Fire Roasted Red Pepper Sauce | 124 |
| Sneaky Hot Ginger Brisket | 125 |
| Braised Brisket-in-a-Bag | 126 |
| Wild Sides: Sweet and Sour Refrigerator Pickles | 126 |

# The Tougher End: Slow Cookers, Pot Roasts, Soups and Stews

| | |
|---|---|
| Laurel and Chuck's Chuck Roast Sandwich Meat | 128 |
| Tips & Tactics: Slow Cooking the Safe Way | 128 |
| Even Better Sandwich Roast | 129 |
| Tips & Tactics: Better Browning for Better Flavor | 129 |
| Easy Tex-Mex Pulled Venison | 130 |
| | |
| Cream of Mushroom Slow Cooker Pot Roast | 131 |
| Tips & Tactics: Why Slow Cook? | 131 |
| Alfredo Pot Roast and Sandwich Meat | 132 |
| Old World Slow-Cooker Ale Roast | 133 |
| Wild Sides: Traditional Potato Salad | 133 |
| | |
| Fall-Apart Oven Pot Roast | 134 |
| Wild Sides: Scalloped Pineapple | 134 |
| Pot Roast with Sour Cream Gravy | 135 |
| Sauer Pot Roast | 136 |
| Slow-Cooker Venison Stroganoff | 137 |
| | |
| Hunter's Hot Pot | 138 |
| Wild Sides: Put a Lid on It | 138 |
| Rib-Sticking Stew | 139 |
| Too Much to Stew Stew | 140 |
| Boone's Stew | 141 |
| | |
| Meredith's Secret Ingredient Stew | 142 |
| All Day Beer Stew | 143 |
| Tips & Tactics: Deglazing the Pan | 143 |
| Wild Rice and Red Wine Hot Pot | 144 |

Slice Of The Wild

# Tough and Tougher: Burger

| | |
|---|---|
| Wild-Tamer Hamburgers | 146 |
| Tips & Tactics: Avoiding the Dreaded Crumbleburger | 146 |
| Garden Burgers | 147 |
| Wild Sides: Mexican Rice | 147 |
| Burgers with Super Catsup | 148 |
| | |
| Wild Sides: Country-Style Potato Salad | 148 |
| Spiced Burger Skewers | 149 |
| Wild Sides: Roundup Salad | 149 |
| Date-Night Burgers with Mushroom Sauce | 150 |
| Wild Sides: Sweet Rice | 150 |
| | |
| Pseudo Corn Dogs | 151 |
| Wild Sides: Curried Potato Salad | 151 |
| Easy Meaty Chili | 152 |
| Wild Sides: Wrap It Up | 152 |
| Rib-Sticking Meatloaf | 153 |
| | |
| Wild Sides: Clean-Oven Onions | 153 |
| Swedish Meatballs | 154 |
| Meatball Wedgies | 155 |
| Mexican Lasagna | 156 |
| Baked Ziti | 157 |
| | |
| Meatballs and Spaghetti | 158 |
| 1-2-3 Tortilla Pie | 159 |
| Wild Variations: Taco Salad & Nacho Chips | 159 |
| Mexican Meatballs and Rice | 160 |
| Easy Mexican Albondigas | 161 |
| Smoked Meatloaf | 162 |

# Tough and Tougher: Sausage and Jerky

| | |
|---|---|
| Breakfast Sausage | 164 |
| Tips & Tactics: Taste Testing Safety | 164 |
| Second Breakfast-in-a-Pot | 165 |
| Christmas Chorizo | 166 |
| Southwestern Egg Rolls | 167 |
| Polish Sausage | 168 |
| | |
| Wild Sides: Josh's Sweet Potato Salad | 168 |
| Butte, America Sausage | 169 |
| Wild Sides: Potato Pancakes | 169 |
| Un-Smoked Smoky Sausage | 170 |
| Wild Sides: Braised Red Cabbage | 170 |
| Easy Italian Sausage | 171 |
| Brats | 172 |
| | |
| Wild Sides: Easy Refrigerator Mustard Pickle | 172 |
| Brats-in-a-Pot Soup | 173 |
| Cajun Sausage | 174 |
| Hoppin' John | 175 |
| Oven Salami | 176 |
| Smoked Fajita Jerky | 177 |
| Trickery Hickory Jerky | 178 |
| | |
| Tips & Tactics: The Best Cuts for Jerky | 178 |
| Zesty Old World Jerky | 179 |
| Mexican Mole Jerky | 180 |
| Pepper Sticks | 181 |
| Biltong-Style Jerky | 182 |
| Tips & Tactics: When Is It Done? | 182 |
| Summer Jerky | 183 |

# No More Mystery Meat

I looked up the word "coping" in the dictionary today. It's a word that invariably shows up every hunting season in our newspapers, embedded in the phrase, Coping with Game Meat. Turns out there are at least two definitions. The first is 'to struggle or deal, especially on fairly even terms or with some degree of success;' the second is 'to face and deal with responsibilities, problems, or difficulties, especially successfully or in a calm or adequate manner.' Oddly, a correct form of the word cope is copelessness, which sounds so much like hopelessness that I have to assume the folks writing those coping with game meat articles must feel a certain amount of it.

My frustration is that I've always used a very different verb--relish--when I refer to game meat. Oh, sure, copelessness applies when trying to get a half ton of elk out of the woods by yourself on a warm September day. But these articles are never about the dragging and the field dressing. They're about the eating, and if that's when they started worrying about eating their game meat, well, they were a few days late. It starts at the shot. Depending on the weather, you may cope on fairly even terms--or not; and you may be able to act in a calm and adequate manner, and you may even be able to up the ante on 'adequate,' managing to enhance and improve the natural flavor and tenderness of the animal lying at your feet. At the very least however, doing no harm.

Slice of The Wild walks you through the journey, from the moment of the shot to the triumph at the table, with lots of photos and time-honored tips to make game care and butchering straightforward and easily accomplished in a modest urban or suburban kitchen. There are no mysteries, no hard and fast rules about what gets cut into what, no expensive tools to buy, no need for game processors, and certainly no need for copelessness.

Little white packages from the game processor may be the easy way to cope with game meat, but when something doesn't taste right, a dish that always worked suddenly doesn't, there's a gap in your knowledge--and your chances of fixing the problem. My mother, who doesn't understand why I hunt, once asked me, "How do you know where it's been?". She was referring to the mess out there in the woods. Me, I worry about once the animal is in my possession. People have stopped and asked me why their whitetail was gamy or their deer tough; if the animal was not in your possession from the moment of the shot until the dish didn't work, you can't possibly pinpoint the problem--or cure it.

But the other part of this book is customizing your meat cutting. We don't all need to feed a family of four; or if we did once, perhaps we don't anymore. Our needs change and so should the way we cut our game animals.

Buy this book. And use it. (Perhaps I should have plastic-coated the pages on custom cutting hind quarters; feel free to copy them and do that.) The methods are simple ones John and I have used for over 30 years. They will make your game as delicious as it can be so that your verb--and meals--will lean toward relishing rather than copelessness. And you'll never pay for processing again.

Slice Of The Wild

# Top Ten Tips For Trophy Eats

## Adrenaline Is A Great Aid When Fleeing; Not So Good As A Marinade

Lots of research has been done on this topic, both on game and commercially raised animals. The more the animal is stressed before death, the more adrenaline, the higher the pH, the less tender and more chewy the animal can become. It's called 'dark cutting.' Higher pH in the meat makes the meat darker, and the surface dryer and slightly sticky to the touch. Some of this we can prevent, some we can't.

Bucks chasing does to the wee hours, before you even wake up, is pretty much unavoidable. But chasing antelope, or organizing whitetail drives aggressive enough to make animals wild-eyed with panic, is an evil marinade you can avoid. It happens in a nanosecond—a very quick marinade. So, if you're in it for the meat, the best shot is a clean shot, with the animal totally unaware of your presence.

The only good thing about higher pH is that dark cutting meat, when ground into burger, tends to stick together and retain moisture better. Otherwise all it does is bad: it risks worse flavor, tougher chewing, as well as faster bacterial growth. (And aging doesn't always remedy that toughness.)

The other factor that causes 'dark cutting' is a shortage of glycogen just before taking the animal. When frightened, adrenaline transforms the glycogen in our livers into glucose, and releases it into the bloodstream. Simply put, glucose is sugar coursing through our veins for a quick burst of energy.

But run long enough, and the body runs out of glucose-producing glycogen. And there you are: what's left produces dark cutting and all its bad effects on meat.

Slice Of The Wild

# Cool It Down In The First 2-4 Hours

Once the animal is down the clock is running. The carcass needs to cool down to 50 degrees or less in 2 to 4 hours. Don't let the carcass sit in the sun, don't wrap it in a blue tarp, don't let freshly killed animals lie cheek to jowl. (Need I say don't drape it across the hood of your vehicle?) All that prevents body heat from escaping.

Do hang the carcass in a cooler, cool garage, or in the shade of some trees. In warmer weather, do split the pelvis and the sternum, and cut the windpipe out, propping open the chest with a long stick. Larger animals always take longer to cool down than smaller ones; at the same temperatures, an elk or moose will need more measures than a whitetail doe to make sure the cooling down is timely and effective.

With larger animals, like moose, elk and larger bucks, it's more important to open the shoulder/neck area; contrary to popular opinion, it's the shoulders that sour before the hind quarters. You can split the pelvis and really separate the hind quarters for good air circulation, but the front quarters are harder to separate. You need to split the sternum (or breastbone) all the way up, and remove the head and neck at the base of the neck to allow good air flow around the shoulder meat. That means carrying a bone saw for the sternum. On small animals, like forkhorn whitetails, I've popped the ribs from the sternum with my pocket knife, but with larger or mature animals, you may need a bone saw to separate ribs from sternum.

Meat processors generally say if the air temperature is 60°F or more, you need to find a cooler at 40°F, or just over freezing, within the first 2 hours. We once disturbed a red-tailed hawk eating his breakfast in a little cluster of cottonwood trees—he'd caught a jack rabbit—to borrow his bit of shade for a fresh antelope kill. I'd taken the buck at first light, and didn't want to delay my partner's hunt. The buck cooled down nicely in the deep morning shade and yes, the ambient air temperature was quite a bit less than 60°F. However, the afternoon was going to be warmer, so when we broke for lunch we transferred the buck to a root cellar on the ranch. The buck was cool to the touch, and in rigor mortis. From there it was important to keep it cool and clean until the carcass relaxed again.

# Aging Helps

All warm-blooded animals have collagen. Some have very little, like antelope. Some have a lot. And some cuts have more than others. Older animals that have exercised more have more complex collagen, which is what makes that meat tougher than younger animals, and forequarters and shanks (the lower leg) have more collagen naturally which is why they are tougher than cuts higher on the animal, like tenderloins. Chilled storage—or aging— helps break down some of this collagen. It's the microscopic connective tissue at the cellular level that's actually being changed, not the meat.

Just for the record, game animals aren't the only ones that get aged. The most expensive restaurants in the world serve aged beef. (It's why they charge so much.) The best are aged up to 30 days at 36°F. To keep prices down, the processors that supply our local supermarkets don't age meat. Aging requires space and time; things that add cost.

The problem is there are still a lot of people who think aging is 'rotting' the meat. Or that it has no effect at all because game meat simply isn't like beef. Hogwash. In countries where game is harvested for the table, and sold in grocery stores, they follow the same procedures described here and they age the meat for tenderness, because consumer survey after consumer survey has shown that the number one quality customers want in their meat is tenderness.

We did an experiment this year. John shot a 6x6 elk late in the season. We took the front—in him quite chewy—half of the tenderloin and put it in a plastic bag in the fridge. Then, every two to three days, we ate a little of it. The change in tenderness was noticeable, especially after one week; after two weeks, we'd plateaued out. He was a bull after all. We'd improved him to the point that an overnight marinade made him pretty tender, but he'd never be a spike. On the other hand, my friend Chris Madson was lucky enough to kill a young elk close to home last fall but was so relieved at that happening, he cut it up the next day. In rigor, he admits now. He says what should have been fork tender is now definitely chewy.

Still arguing with your friends whether to hang big game animals head up or head down? You're both wrong. According to the people who study these things, the best way to hang 4-legged animals is by the pelvis, essentially as they stand, keeping muscle groups stretched, in the same position they were on the hoof. (We hang them head down.)

How much chilled storage? It depends on the temperature. Since most hunters don't have commercial coolers, we work with the ambient air temperature. In early season, when temperatures are warmer, just getting the animal past rigor is often aging enough. In late season, when temperatures hover at freezing and below, if you can keep the carcass from freezing, and it still has its skin on to keep the meat from drying out, two weeks of hanging is not too much.

So when you figure the costs of hunting and how much you're saving by providing your own meat, factor in the higher priced aged meat served in fancy restaurants instead of the price charged at your local super market. That is, if you do age your game. According to the most scientific journals, you really have upgraded it.

## Larger Is Better

Meat that's boned out right away gets tougher in rigor mortis than meat left attached--and stretched the length of the bone--because once you cut those attachments, there's nothing to keep it from contracting. Scientists call it 'muscle shortening.' The more the muscle is allowed to contract, the tougher the meat, and even long, careful aging won't stretch it back out. If you have to carry an animal out on your back, the larger you can keep the pieces of meat the better. Hanging the animal whole keeps muscles stretched and works best against muscle-shortening; quartering is second best; boning out the meat, but leaving the muscle lengths whole is third best; reducing the meat to chunks, especially while in rigor mortis, is asking for trouble.

## Rigor Affects Tenderness

There's an old rural legend about the hunter who flops his deer into the trunk of his car, right after he's shot and dressed it, only to arrive home a few hours later with the animal literally frozen in place. That's rigor mortis: Latin for the 'stiffness of death.' All warm blooded animals go through rigor, birds as well as big game animals. In warm weather it happens fairly quickly, in cold more slowly. It's hard to predict the timing, but easy to tell what's happening. Rigor has not started when the animal is loosey-goosey; it's in rigor when it's stiff and unbending; and done when the joints once again can be bent. (Not as easily as before rigor, but enough to manipulate the joints for skinning and butchering.) If you cut, wrap, and freeze the meat when it's in rigor it will be tougher than waiting the day or so longer it takes to be completely out. Scientists call it 'thaw rigor,' when you freeze an animal during rigor. It can happen on frigid hunts, when you don't intend it; and when you process meat and freeze it too soon after the kill. Let rigor run it's course before processing, and you'll have more tender meat.

### What does rigor look like?

This pheasant is an easily handled example. It was a warm afternoon--shirtsleeve weather. We'd shot this guy, stretched him out on the bed of the shaded pick-up, and hunted another hour. When we got back, he was in rigor, exactly as we'd left him. And no, I'm not holding him that way. He's balancing on my open palm: so stiff I could use him for a game of darts.

When we set out the next morning, his head was drooping--coming out of rigor. It had taken about 16 hours at an average temperature of 45°F. Not long. But had we butchered him during that 16 hours, we'd have been chewing a lot longer.

# Cleanliness Is Next To Goodliness

Except for adrenaline, the worst things to marinate your meat in are blood, viscera, and dirt. When you're done field dressing an animal, lift it up as high as possible to drain all the blood and offal. Then rinse the body cavity with clean water, or several armfuls of snow when available. If you don't have help to lift the animal high, simply turn it over a bush or log, and let the blood drain. Then rinse. A 5-gallon jug or two of water for game care should be as basic as a tire iron and second spare tire for hunting truck equipment.

As soon as you get home, or somewhere with clean running water, check the body cavity again, and rinse it again if necessary. Then hang the animal in a clean, cool, dry place. In hotter early season weather, especially if you're a long way from home, check with the local meat processor to see if he'll just hang your animal to cool it down, without processing. Usually they charge a minimal fee, and it's well worth it when the ambient temperature hovers around 70 or above. In Montana, we have low humidity, so even if hunting days are warm, nights cool off. In more humid parts of the country, you can't count on those cooler nights, so meat coolers are even more important.

A good, clean heart/lung shot will keep you way forward of the viscera and avoid that contamination. Leaving the skin on protects the outside from dirt and debris. The skin acts as a sterile dressing until you pull it off. Pulling it off after the animal is hung in a clean garage will keep the meat cleaner than if you had to skin it in the field. Keeping the skin on also keeps the carcass from drying out. Thus, you'll trim—and waste—less meat during butchering. So don't skin the animal in the field unless there is no other way to cool it down.

# Removing The Scent Gland—Or Not.

Not long ago, everyone removed the scent gland as a matter of course. It's not necessary. In fact, I've never done it, and I've never felt that the glands contaminated the meat, nor has anyone I've ever fed our game meat to complained of an off flavor. Believe me, I'm as sensitive to gamy flavors as anyone you know.

However, if you do remove the glands and then take that same knife and touch the meat with it, you're actually doing harm. That gland secretion is an oil and only soap and water will remove it all from the knife—and your hands. Wipe it in snow and dry it on your wool pants, and you'll end up contaminating every piece of meat your knife touches.

## Chest Freezers Are Best

It really does make a difference whether you use a chest, upright, or refrigerator freezing compartment. For one thing chest freezers are colder and don't lose cold when opened. Since cold falls (and heat rises) the cold stays put in a chest freezer even after 5 or 10 minutes of the door being open; in an upright or refrigerator/freezer compartment, the cold falls out immediately. The constant up and down of temperature causes moisture to evaporate from the meat. If the temperature fluctuates often enough, the meat surface turns brown and scaly: freezer burn. If you wrap loosely, there will also be a tell-tale snow drift inside the package where the moisture condensed and was trapped, against the inside of the freezer paper. Wrapping tightly in freezer paper, or with plastic wrap before wrapping in freezer paper helps prevent this, as does vacuum sealing. A chest freezer goes that much farther at keeping frozen meat fresher.

The other factor in freezing meat is that the faster it freezes, the better the outcome. Don't try to freeze more than 1 ½ pounds of meat per 1 square foot of freezer space: that's 22 pounds of meat in the average 15 square foot freezer. Most deer-sized animals yield a little more than that in boned meat, so if you have two freezers, spread it out. Otherwise, it helps to layer the warm meat between already frozen packages: layering on metal cookie sheets speeds the process, too. Then, check the progress after 24 hours, and rotate the coldest with the warmest packages.

What's the freezer life of game? It's the same as for commercial meat. In a chest freezer, at 0° to -5°F, in snugly wrapped, intact packaging, whole roasts and steaks will keep for 6 to 8 months or longer. Ground meat, especially with fat added, lasts about half that. Double wrapping extends freezer life; and only grinding as much burger as you'll use in 3 to 4 months keeps your burger fresher. If you have trouble organizing chest freezers, look to Moving Day (in the Custom Cutting section). John and I rarely have trouble finding what we're looking for.

## Keep It Simple

Processing used to be a simple act, designed to please a small audience. It still can be. With a couple of knives, a little paper, and a marking pen—and just a little bit of knowledge of anatomy—you can eliminate much of the hocus-pocus of butchering. Everyone thinks wild game animals are full of bugs. But it's the big-business processing of commercial meats that we should worry about instead. The Center for Disease Control estimates there are 1 1/2 million cases of foodborne illness each year—at a minimum. (Most aren't reported—or officially diagnosed.) Not all of that is meat caused, but a significant percentage is. Wild animals don't live in close quarters, like cattle in a feedlot. They're not fed growth agents and hormones, parasitics, antibiotics and a steady dose of fattening corn. Do your own processing and you eliminate the question marks: one animal at a time; only your animals on the cutting board, ever. If we are what we eat, we should know what we are.

Our government spends billions each year trying to keep our meat safe; there is a more efficient way. Let those who will eat it, be the ones who process it. Amazing how picky we get then.

## Keep It Red

The fastest way to ruin meat--any meat--is to overcook it. Anyone who's ever suffered through an overcooked Christmas turkey knows what I'm talking about. Meat gets dry when you overcook it, but the worst thing is that the flavors get concentrated--since the water that diluted the flavors is now gone. Leave a little moisture--and a little red, even if it's only a pink red--and you will have better game meals. Trust me. We have fed antelope to people who hate antelope, mule deer to people who hate mule deer, and game in general to people who are die-hard beef-eaters. They all ask for seconds, as they ask what did you do to it. The answer is as little as possible, and at the same time, as much as necessary. But number one is always: don't overcook it.

## One More Word

These tips are a result of years of very pointed research in scientific books and journals, including: Meat Science: The Official Journal of the American Meat Science Association, Meat Science and Applications by Y.H. Yui; Recent Advances in the Chemistry of Meat: The proceedings of a symposium; International Congress of Meat Science and Technology, Quality Attributes of Muscle Foods edited by Youling L. Xiong, Chi-Tang Ho and Fereidoon Shahidi and other sources clipped, stacked and lost over the years which were then applied and adapted to our own dressing, cooling, aging and cutting, cooking and timing methods.

What we read we tested, and what worked stuck. More than one long-time hunter has refused to believe we'd served them their least favorite game meat. Some refused to believe we'd served them game at all. One Midwestern whitetail hunter, after staying with us for several days, commented that we treated our game as if it was real meat. It is. And when it is treated that way, it is a joy to eat.

From the field to the table, we try to make game handling easy, consistent, and efficient. The most basic rule is once the game is on the ground, do no harm. Beyond that, we strive to enhance the best of what we have, and make those packets of game meat in our freezer as tender and tasty as we can.

If you and your family are happy with the way your game meat tastes and chews, and the time it takes to get from field to freezer, keep doing what you're doing. If not, turn the page and give our methods a try.

# Field To Gambrel
## Field Care

# The Devil Is In The Details: Taking It Apart

How many and what kind of pieces you cut your big game animal into is totally up to you. Some people prefer burger, and will grind the whole animal up with either no beef suet or up to 30% suet added. Others prefer steaks and will find every bit of available steak potential on the carcass. At our house, we've gone through stages. These days it seems we run through the steaks and burger fastest. When my son was a teenager, and had a great big protein hunger, we cut more roasts. It was the only way to provide him with all the meat he craved. (Some days entire elk rump roasts would disappear into that boy. But he was growing fast, and he needed it.) We still cut roasts these days, both tougher shoulder cuts for pot roasting and more tender hind quarter cuts for dry roasting, for company and lazy weekends. (You know: cook once, graze forever?) But there are a few things that don't change whether you're a family of two watching your waistline, or a family with teenagers. The hunter still has to get the animal to the cook either at least as good as, but perhaps in better shape, than it was when standing on its own four feet.

Finally, if you've leafed through the recipe section already, you'll notice there are no special sections for elk, deer, or antelope, just recipes for big game. All big game. For the better part of three decades John and I have played the "Who are you eating?" game. (Norm and Sil Strung taught us the game, and had played it years before that.) Despite the fact that we eat game every day, we're only right about 25% of the time. (And in a way, we're cheating, because we know what's in our freezer.) It's a matter of degree sometimes, not so radical as chicken vs. beef, or tofu vs. turkey. It's all red meat, and the tastes vary some, but the details that are most important for the cook have less to do with who we're eating, than what cut we're eating, how large is it, and how good was that field care. Big old moose or diminutive whitetail, you can cut all the steaks and roasts to a uniform size, if that's what you want; and if you grade and label your meat carefully, you can eliminate the other variables. Beyond that, field care has the most effect on how hard the cook has to work. Let's give the cook a hand.

## Clean And Cool

In a perfect world, the woods would not be where I choose to field dress an animal, but that's where we are when field dressing needs to be done. Because as important as cleanliness is, time is of the essence. For the mildest flavor, it's best to field dress the animal as soon as it hits the ground, then to rinse any dirt, blood, or debris off the inside of the carcass with clean, cold water. If clean snow is all that's available, it will melt as soon as it hits the carcass, so that works as well. When we're hunting in dry country, we carry at least two 5-gallon jugs of water for this purpose. Water from lakes, streams and rivers will work, unless you're hunting somewhere like Alaska, during a salmon run, when the streams are full of dying fish and bacteria. Once dressed, get the animal cooled down to as close to 40°F as possible within 2 to 4 hours.

# Frigid Game Care

While cold weather is often a blessing to safe meat handling, frigid weather--10° to 20° below zero-- is a problem. Cold inhibits the speed of rigor mortis; it takes longer to go in, and longer yet to go out than on warmer days, and if the carcass freezes while it's in rigor, it often results in tougher meat. At worst the only cure is the grinder. At best, that naturally tender forkhorn will chew like an old buck. Slow cooking or marinating won't completely cure it, so if you're unlucky enough to be hunting in such cold weather, try your best to keep the animal from freezing solid within 24 to 36 hours of the kill.

At home, we have a wood stove in the garage where we hang meat. In the field, we cut the animal into quarters and stow it in a large cooler--one of those 100 quart marine coolers people often refer to as 'striper coffins.' They not only insulate stuff from heat, but they're very good at insulating stuff from freezing. (Plus they're long enough to fit a full length deer or elk quarter in, so you don't lose the stretching effect of leaving the animal in quarters, and attached to the bone.) Just be sure you don't over-insulate; you still need to complete the basic cooling in 2-4 hours. Crack the cooler lid at first so you don't trap the heat. Then touch the quarters, every hour on the hour, until you're sure they're cool enough. A minimum body temperature of 50°F--32 to 38°F is ideal--will keep bacteria in check. (The carcass should feel quite cold to the touch.) As with everything related to food safety, keep your eyes and olfactory senses alert. Once you get tuned in, you'd be amazed what they'll tell you. (Just remember the last time you walked by the 'fresh' fish counter at your local supermarket. I'm sure your nose was telling you that their fish were several days deader than the ones in your creel last summer.)

# Aging Meat

A lot of folks say they don't age their meat, but a lot of folks kill forkhorn bucks and hunt more than 24 hours from their homes. By the time they get those critters out of the woods, down the road, and to the cutting table, they've 'aged' on their own. And if this was a planned week long hunt, and they killed the animal on the first or second day, they've aged a lot.

We've always aged everything from young whitetail does to big bull moose. For the older animals, it makes the meat more tender. For the younger ones, it makes the flavor less bland. (Yes, whitetail does are bland.) Last fall John killed a moose; since we had been pretty lucky last fall, we decided to share the wealth, splitting the animal down the spine and dropping off one half with a couple of friends. They also butcher their own meat and were very happy to get it.

We took our half home and hung it in the garage to age for several days. Our friends butchered the next day. Same animal, same cuts, same care to a point; but the moose at our house is more tender and the flavor is more mellow and complex. That's what aging does.

The safest temperature to age meat at is about 38° to 40°F. We have aged meat at that temperature for 2-3 weeks; when we aged that moose, it hovered between 40° to 50°F so we only aged him for 1 week. (Some people push it to the first signs of mold; we don't recommend it.) How long you age is totally dependent on the temperature; the end results are totally dependent on how diligently you watch the animal. Check morning and evening; in warmer weather, check at noon as well. If you have any doubts, start cutting and wrapping. But if you can let your game age, you gain tenderness and taste. Even a couple of days helps: a Cree moose guide once pointed out that freshly killed game meat, eaten right away, produces more flatulence than aged meat. In his experience, a minimum of 48 hours was necessary just for that factor. We like to take ours past the flatulence factor.

John and I live in Montana, but we've also hunted in warmer, wetter climates. My least favorite hunt, just for the issue of game care, was a mid-March visit to Alabama. It was 90° the whole time. Uncomfortable for the hunter, difficult for game care. In places like that, it pays to invest in a cooler, root cellar or another device to ensure that your animal cools down in that first 2 to 4 hours. You just can't depend on the cold night air to do the work. It doesn't get cold enough. And it also doesn't get dry enough to get a good hard crust on the meat as it ages. (That's one thing fancy restaurants look for.) The air is so moist that mold is much more of a problem. And mold is never a good thing. If you are aging meat, and see mold, even one spore, get out the knives immediately and process that animal. Some will rinse the mold off with a bleach/water solution; but recent evidence suggests that the mold you see is only the beginning. Don't wash, cut. Cut away the mold, trim away anything questionable. And freeze. That alone puts the end to mold.

It's time to cut. We've always butchered in the kitchen, partly because hunting season gets pretty cold in Montana, but also because we have no running water in the garage, and cleanliness is important, too. Finished cuts should be clean: no hair, no blood, no crusty bits, no leaves, no dirt. We always start by cleaning away as much hair and debris as we can before we start quartering and cutting. It's always easier and more efficient to wipe larger chunks than smaller.

## How Do They Taste?

John and I have an ongoing conflict. He likes hunting mule deer on the plains. I prefer whitetail on river bottoms. But we agree on what we like to eat best. Moose might be number one, with whitetail and antelope right behind. But we also like caribou and mule deer, when they're taken at the right time of year. You'll notice elk's not on the top of the list. That's because over the years we've noticed more variation in elk flavor and texture than any other game animal we've hunted. The broken off 5-point John took one September first was one of the best animals we've ever had in the freezer; the 6x6 he took in British Columbia was definitely bland. Not gamy, but so off-puttingly bland that he needed as much marinating as a gamy animal; and the cow we took on Priscilla's Knob was more like liver than elk meat. Again, she wasn't gamy, but we often wondered if she'd had too rich a diet. After all, we all are what we eat.

On the other hand, we've never had a spike we didn't like. And after surveying our elk-hunting friends, we've discovered that our experience isn't unusual. In fact, we didn't find anyone who had anything bad to say about spikes. We suspect it's because they aren't sexually active yet, so they're not running around like an over-sexed chicken, nor do they have the nutritional drain of nursing a calf. Spikes have the full complement of simple poundage, without the burdens of adulthood. That 5-point John took in Colorado last year was very good, as was a heifer I took a while ago. But it is simply much more predictable, before the shot, to know what you're going to get with a spike: they are going to be quite tasty and tender. The rest—cows and bulls of all ages—vary from animal to animal without predictable pattern.

Moose is almost always good, and we've talked with folks in Canada and Alaska for whom moose is the constant in their freezer who say the same thing. The only bad moose I've ever eaten was a trophy Shiras taken at the end of the season, he tasted fine, but was quite tough. I wasn't in on the kill. The moose ended up at a friend's house, I was there, so I helped butcher, and was given some shoulder meat in thanks. Now shoulder isn't the most tender meat, but I also didn't and don't know what his game care routine was. Moose, hunter, or just bad luck? If you're not there from the opening credits, it's hard to tell why it tastes or chews the way it does.

Males of the mule deer, caribou, and elk persuasion all suffer from a rutty gaminess eventually. When they are rutting, the meat suffers. If you're in it for the trophy, you'll just have to make sausage, because the rut makes the big boys forget about sleeping and eating properly. But if you're in it for the meat, hunt them pre-rut or early in the rut, then lay off until the rut is well over, when they have a chance to put some weight back on again.

Bighorn sheep rams, are almost always muttony in the rut, but can be quite tasty before the rut; and ewe meat is good, too. The fat is the problem. It has to be stripped ruthlessly before cooking. Ribs for instance need to be parboiled to render all the fat off, but muscle meat, once trimmed very well, can be cooked with any of the recipes in this book. To me, good bighorn meat is a cross between whitetail and commercial lamb, not lamby enough to warrant mint jelly, but given the right young ewe, a great candidate for grilling or kabobs. Rams not taken in the rut can be just as good.

Good mule deer meat is a joy to eat. And to me, good caribou is as good as good mule deer. (John doesn't think caribou taste at all like mule deer.) But both need to be taken when they're not rutting, and for mule deer that makes trophy hunting a lot trickier.

I hesitate to call antelope 'delicate,' but they seem most sensitive to our bad handling. If they're run before the shot, if they're not cooled down properly after the shot, they can be absolutely rank. The trick is to shoot them unawares, and to cool them down within 2-4 hours of the kill to that optimum 40°F. Sometimes it's a struggle: antelope season always has some warm, sunny weather, and you're often a long way from civilization. You just need to plan ahead: two 5-gallon water jugs and a large cooler; then a skinning and fillet knife in case you need to quarter him out. Carry enough ice so you can stuff two bags of block ice high in the body cavity, then drape another 2 or 3 bags of cube ice over the top of the shoulders and hind quarters. (Remember, cold falls; a little ice underneath helps, but more should be placed on top.) And keep the ice bagged so he doesn't end up a soupy mess.

John and I have butchered or helped butcher over 200 animals—including a good-sized herd of antelope. Of all those animals, we've had two randy, trophy mule deer (no mystery there) and one bad pronghorn buck. It was in Wyoming, on a guided hunt. John shot a buck, we gutted it, and handed it over to our guide who swore he'd take it straight back to the ranch and hang it in the cooler. He didn't. Instead, he wrapped it tightly in a blue tarp so it wouldn't drip on his clean vehicle, and then drove around for 2 hours with it in the back of his SUV, baking in the sun. Eventually, it made good sausage.

Antelope are like whitetail in that the bucks don't get that rank, nasty flavor after they've been rutting hard. Mule deer, bull elk, and caribou can get that way, but not whitetail and not antelope. It's us. We're the ones who ruin antelope meat. So for all those who complain about antelope tasting gamy, it would be a good idea to re-evaluate your field care. Remember: first, do no harm.

Now, before you start butchering that animal hanging in the garage, here's a rogues' gallery of sorts: the best and the worst of game animals we've taken.

Rogues' Gallery: What did they taste like?

## Mule Deer

Let's start with mule deer, because some of us hunt them in the rut, and that can really affect flavor. All the animals on the facing page were taken in Montana or Wyoming during our respective rifle seasons, October and November. Field care was the same in each case, all were aged, all were packaged the same way. Yet the results were very different. One was tough, one was bland, one was incredibly gamey tasting, one was tender and tasty, and one froze--while hanging in the barn--and didn't get butchered up until March.

Can you guess? That one on the upper left is the famous Randy. I shot him on November 17, the very beginning of the rut in Montana, but he was already far gone despite the moderate size of his antlers and neck. We cooked the tenders and high hind quarter roasts with lots of seasoning, but ground the rest for sausage. (And before we ground it up we ruthlessly cut away all the connective tissue: anything you couldn't see through. That's where the real gamy flavors settle in.)

The doe to the right was bland, as many does and immature bucks are--including forkhorns. She didn't need aging for tenderness sake, but aging her turned her from bland to scrumptious.

Rumor has it that stags (males of the deer family with undescended or damaged testicles who can't reproduce nor transition from velvet to hardened antlers) are more tender than most deer, but this one (upper right) was so old, we took a piece of hanging tenderloin for the T & T Test and he still failed. That should have been the most tender part, but it was tough as nails so we ground all of him into burger.

Lower left? I shot this buck just before the rut, took him home and hung him in the barn to age. About 10 days later the Siberian Express descended on Montana, unannounced, and he froze solid. Since I'm allergic to deer hair, we couldn't bring him indoors to thaw, so there he hung. Everyone predicted he'd be ruined, but we just kept going out to the barn and knocking on his hind quarters. As soon as he started thawing, we cut him up. He was delicious. I think what helped was that it was cool enough when I'd shot him that we didn't skin him out. But he aged a few days before he froze, and he had his skin to keep his meat moist during the long winter. Little white packages could not have made a tighter seal, and it didn't seem to make any difference that he was frozen outside the freezer rather than inside it.

That guy in the middle? He was shot in mid-October in Wyoming, well before the rut, and was tender and delicious, fat neck and all. To the right of him, is a photo that's three decades older: John was just a kid then, but he shot that buck before the rut started, too, and knew enough about meat care that he aged him for two weeks. It turned out to be one of John's five best tasting and chewing mule deer.

field to table

rogues' gallery

Whitetail Deer

As rutty as mule deer can be, whitetail meat quality varies little from the beginning of the season to the end of the rut--and beyond.  John's whitetail (left) was taken on November 8th; mine (middle) on November 24. We took them five years apart, but both in the rut, which gets hot in Montana around the 18th of November.  Both were trailing does and paying little attention to self-preservation. Both tasted delicious right down to their toes; and the weather was cold enough--without being frigid--that we aged them a full 2 to 3 weeks just above freezing.  They were as tender as the best beef--and as delicious as the little 4x4 I took November 1, on right, a good two weeks before he was going to even start thinking about the rut.  Note too, that both the bigger bucks were taken in cold weather, while the little one was taken in moderate weather.  (You can tell by the clothing.)  Whitetail is just some of the best wild meat there is.  Dependably.

## Pronghorn Antelope

John's antelope, at left, was the biggest-bodied antelope we'd ever seen shot. After field dressing and three days of drying out--while we hunted a few rooster pheasants--he still weighed 94 pounds. That's monstrous for an antelope. The funny thing was that John thought he was aiming at the biggest doe he'd ever seen; when we walked up on him, we discovered the buck had already lost his sheaths--the 'horn' you see--and was such a trophy that even his cores (the permanent part of his headgear that the sheath sits on) were ivory-tipped. He should have had longer horns than the 14 1/2 inch buck I took, middle, many years ago. Like whitetails, though all this is academic when it comes to eating. As long as the antelope isn't overheated when shot, and is cooled down after the shot, I've never noticed any difference in taste from old trophy bucks to young nubile does--and even non-typicals like the one on the right. Antelope season is often warmer than general rifle seasons, so the cooling down requires more effort, but they all taste good when properly handled. And since antelope have less collagen than other big game animals, there aren't the variations in tenderness. All antelope are created tender. As long as they don't freeze--or you don't butcher--during rigor, they'll stay that way.

field to table

◇

rouges' gallery

The Truth About Elk

You can tell I'm the meat hunter in our family, because I'm the one with the spike elk. A lot of my fellow Montanans think elk is the best meat in the world, but over the years John and I have found that the flavor is variable. Spikes are the most dependably delicious, with small raghorn bulls, like the one in the middle, taking a close second. Big bulls can be very good but they can also get quite run down when rutting, and guessing how long it takes for them to get healthy again--it's a chance you take. Don't get me wrong. Someday, a bull like the one on the top right is going to step out of the woods, and rut or not, I'm going to kill it. In the meantime, I'm very happy when a spike or a little 5-point volunteers a standing broadside shot.

The issue is partly rut gaminess. But there's something else going on with elk, because the cows are just as variable in flavor as the larger bulls. Maybe more so. I've eaten everything from seriously bland bulls to livery cows, and so far haven't been able to pinpoint the specifics. You have to assume it's nutrition and stress, but guessing which elk grazing in my crosshairs has been eating noxious weeds and staying up too late? Give me the young bull, every time.

# Special Permits

## Bighorn Sheep

This ewe was delicious, as was the ewe I shot in 1991; the only problem with bighorn sheep is that you cannot eat the fat. Treat it as you would any game animal, but trim the fat ruthlessly. And don't cook the meat with the fat. If you can't cut it away, parboil it before adding it to anything else. The fat is where the famous muttony flavor lives: the muscle meat is delicious. Like mule deer, elk, and caribou, rams get quite gamy during the rut, but before and after they've recovered can be very good eating.

## Moose

The size is intimidating and makes moose field care a bit daunting, especially in warm weather, but the only bad moose I ever bit into was a chewy trophy Shiras that had been chased around all fall. Then again, I wasn't in on the kill and can't attest to the field care. This one was taken in shirt-sleeve weather, and skinned that evening. We let him hang 5 days at home, in the mid-40's, then butchered him. He was fork tender and very tasty.

## Bison

I took this 2 1/2 year old cow bison in Texas and brought the meat home. It was as tender as the best moose or elk, and even lower in fat. Because of the low fat content, it's best cooked as you would game meat, being careful not to take it much past pink and dry it out.

Slice Of The Wild

field to table

## Musk Ox

John shot this old, run-down musk ox bull, then turned around and gave his guide David a hind quarter and tenderloin. It was no favor. When we got home I discovered that the meat was too tough to even power marinate: the meat dissolved into fibers after 45 minutes on the machine, but the fibers had to be swallowed whole: they were still too tough to chew. I don't know anyone who's ever travelled so far to kill a cow musk ox, but if they're like their brethren the bison and water buffalo that we have eaten, healthy, fat animals would be lots better than this over-the-hill bull.

◇

rogues' gallery

## Caribou

John and I disagree about the flavor of caribou. I think the best caribou is similar to the best mule deer: a distinctive prairie sort of flavor with no gaminess. John thinks they're even better than that and have their own distinctly not-mule deer flavor. The trick to getting good meat is to time your hunt before they go into the rut because caribou get even gamier than mule deer can. It means you'll be hunting with mosquitoes and black flies, but the meat is worth it, there's no trouble cooling it down, and if you are lucky enough to hunt with the Inuits it is an adventure of a lifetime.

# Exotics

No matter where you hunt, everyone has an opinion on what's the best game to eat. Gail, our cook in New Zealand, asked us to take a fallow deer for the table, because that was her favorite, and after we'd grilled it and slathered garlic butter on at the last minute, we all ended up agreeing with her. We had fallow deer again in Ireland after hunting them all day and our host, Liam Kenehan, considered it the best as well. I thought it tasted like the finest of whitetail.

In Namibia, we ate game at every meal: zebra, wildebeest, kudu, springbok, hartebeest, eland, among others, but each was either overcooked or heavily seasoned. It made me want to push the trained chef out of the kitchen and do it myself. But in South Africa this year, our host Keith Gradwell of Kevin Thomas Safaris was into none of that, and treated all of us to a braii—African-style grilling. The hartebeest tasted fine but was a bit chewy, and Keith told us it hadn't been aged as long as he'd like. The kudu, however, was like the mildest elk I'd eaten—rich and beefy in flavor, and fork tender. Keith said he'd aged it, then marinated it all morning in a commercial braai seasoning (which tasted a lot like Gideon's Grub Rub) and oil, and grilled it to a rare to medium rare finish. Most South Africans put the springbok, impala, and eland at the head of their list, but I couldn't imagine how they could be better than that kudu. As we stood around the braai, I asked Keith about game care, and found his was the same as Gail's, Liam's, John's, and mine, except he gets a lot more help. Field dressing, cooling, aging, cleanliness: no matter where you go, no matter what the language, it's the key to good game.

Unfortunately when you hunt in Africa, New Zealand, Europe, and most everywhere else outside of North America you can't bring the game home. But there are exotics in some states now, especially the warmer states like Arizona and Texas. If you take one or more of these exotics, bring the meat home, preferably unprocessed. Then do a quick T & T Test. (If you don't have a shoulder, just pick anything to start with.) My guess is you'll find, as we have that they taste more like our native game than not. After all, red meat is red meat—more similar to each other than to say, chicken. The other universal of game is that it's all lower in fat and exercises more than commercial meat, so has more developed muscle. Given that, it's best to cook exotics with wild game recipes rather than those designed for commercial meat.

And what about buffalo? It's not exotic; it's native and it's raised wild, rather than in feedlots, so it's more like wild game, usually. Free range bison and moose are the lowest in fat of any game animal, less than 1%, and similar to elk in that they all eat grass. (Antelope, for instance, eat forbs.) The biggest difference is that moose and buffalo are bigger than elk, which are bigger than deer, antelope, and caribou, but if you cut your own, you can cut them down to size.

One more thing about exotics: when we hunt them we're usually trophy hunting. So the animals we bring home are older, and perhaps off their feed. I'm sure that's one reason our Namibian cook went to such great lengths to mask the flavor; but as Keith proved, with proper aging, field care, and a light touch cooking, those trophy animals can be quite toothsome and delicious.

Enough about the rest of the world. Do you have an animal hanging in the garage? Let's get to it!

# Field Dressing

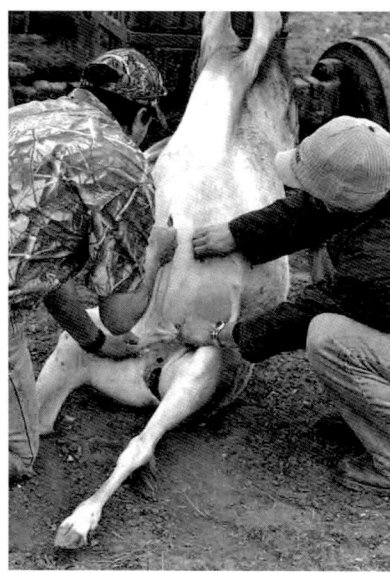 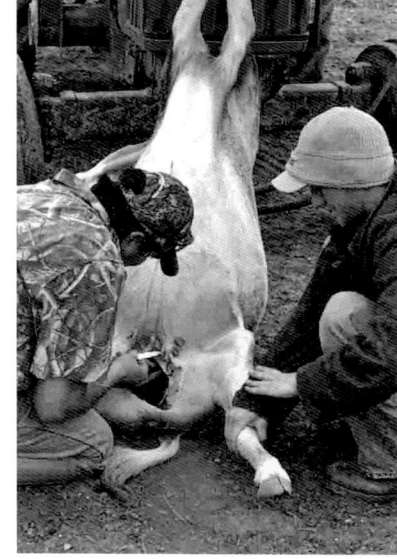 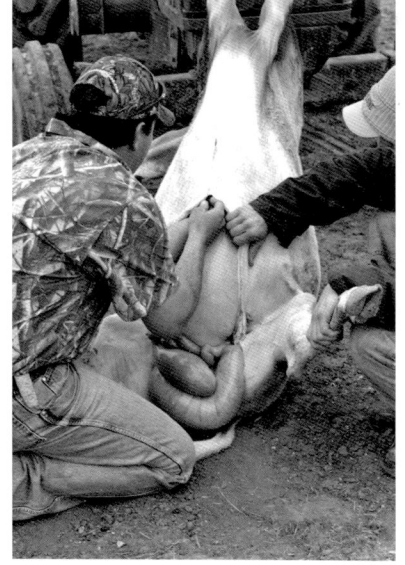

Place the animal belly up on the ground, or hanging from its neck. (In this case, we hung the animal from a front end loader; handy for larger animals, when possible.) Starting at the groin, slice away the udder, or with males, slice between the penis sheath and belly, leaving both attached: flip to the side. Pinch the belly skin up at the navel, and lift it: make a 1 to 2-inch slit in the skin. Insert your knife, edge up, and cut the skin, but not the membrane between skin and viscera, up the center of the belly to the sternum or breast bone.

Come back to the groin, and cut through the membrane, exposing the intestines. Now you have a choice: to remove the intestines safely without contaminating the meat you can either score a hole around the anus (and pull it through the hole once the rest of the viscera is loose) or split the pelvis. When cutting around the anus, make the cut generous to avoid puncturing the colon. For splitting the pelvis, see detailed photos on page 34.

Once you've freed the lower end of the intestinal tract, cut up the belly to the sternum through the membrane holding in the viscera, being careful to not puncture the stomach or any other part of the intestinal tract.

As you cut through the membrane, the guts will start spilling out. As they do, push them out of your way.

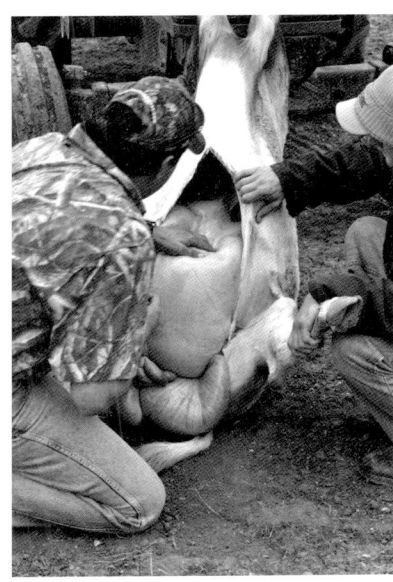 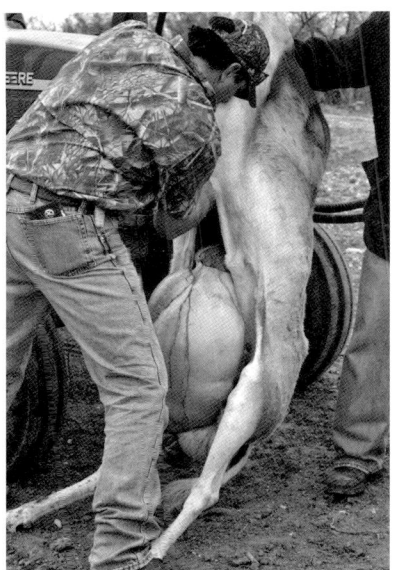 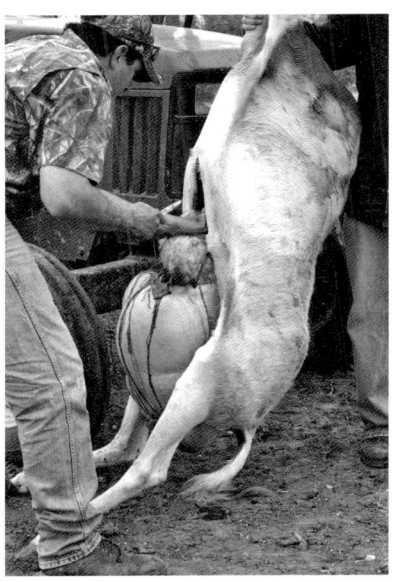

Gently press the paunch down and to one side of the body cavity as you work.

Now, reach inside the upper chest cavity, and find the esophagus, or wind pipe. It's about 2 inches in diameter, with hard rings spaced along its length. Grab hold of it as high as you can in the neck and slice across the esophagus (between the rings) to cut it free.

The esophagus is attached to everything else and is a sturdy handle: for a non-slip hold, make a small slit between 2 rings, so you can hook your finger inside. Now pull, firmly but steadily, cutting away the diaphragm as you go. (It's the thin layer of tissue that attaches to the inside wall of the carcass.) The internal organs will begin to come with the esophagus.

Slice Of The Wild

← Pull and cut, until the viscera are in a pile at your feet or to one side of the carcass. (If some intestinal fluid is leaking, from either bullet or knife wound, try to prevent that fluid from getting on the meat as you move the viscera out.) Then move it to the side, so you can finish the job. Did you cut around the anus? Gently draw the end of the intestines back into the carcass through the hole you've made. If the end of the tract doesn't come easily, carefully slice away any connective tissue until the lower tract is free.

Move the animal away from the gut pile; if you were field dressing on the ground as is most likely, lift the animal by the antlers or shoulders, and drain the blood from the body cavity. Rinse the body cavity out with clean water or clean snow, until there is no dirt or debris, and no puddles of blood. There really isn't much difference between this photo at left and the ones before. If you're lucky, you have a front end loader to help with field dressing but most often field dressing is done far from mechanized help. It doesn't matter where or how, it all needs to be done—cleanly, neatly and as quickly as possible. Remember, what happens here ends up on your fork.

## Splitting the Pelvis

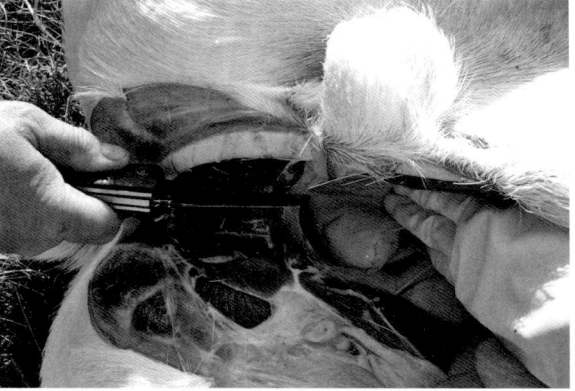
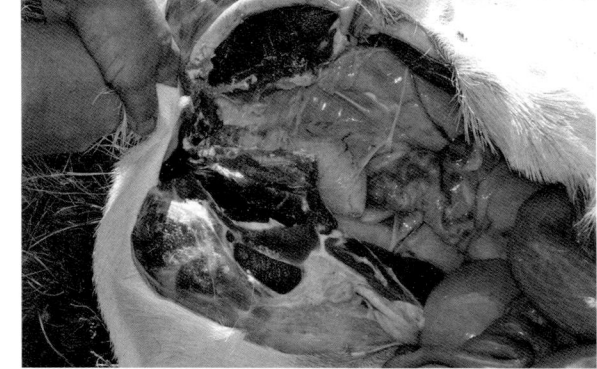

↑ Do you always cut around the anus and pull it back through the body cavity? Splitting the pelvis, or hipbone, keeps the anus outside the belly cavity so you don't risk contamination. Here's how. With the lower intestines moved outside the body cavity, saw through the pelvis. A 4-inch saw on your Swiss Army knife is enough to do this job.

↗ Then place one foot on each hind quarter, and give the tail a jerk up. That will open the pelvis wide enough to draw the lower intestines and urethra through with no danger of contaminating the meat. It also allows the hind quarters to cool down more easily since they're now splayed wide apart.

# Hanging, Splitting, and Aging

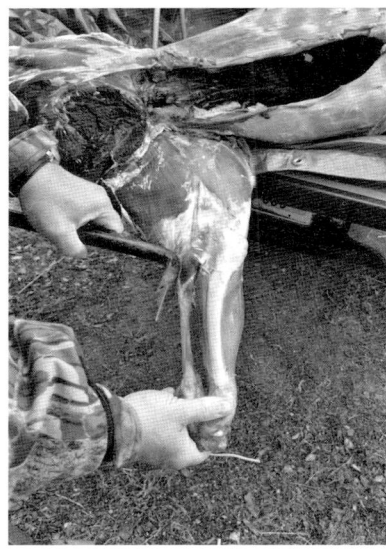

## To Hang an Animal

← A lot of people hang animals from the antlers (or neck). That's okay if it's cold, and you don't need to quarter the animal to get it home. But if it's warm, you may need to remove the head and neck--to allow the front quarters to cool down more quickly. So a good, dependable anchor point on the other end of the animal is crucial. Luckily big game animals have one. It's on the hind leg, just above the ankle joint.

Start by cutting through the skin, 360° around the leg, just below the ankle. I know that looks like the knee by John's right hand, but it's really the ankle. Just above it are the tibia and the fibula--or shin bones. Not the humerus.) Pull the hide back to expose the tendon that attaches from the back of the ankle to the knee. It's a very tough tendon: poke your knife into the space between the tendon and bone large enough to insert a gambrel, rope or whatever you'll use to hang the animal. Repeat for the other back leg.

← Once the gambrel is inserted through both legs, you can use a winch or come-along to hang the animal from the meat pole.

# Splitting the Carcass

While most deer and antelope can be transported whole, larger animals are easier to handle if you take the carcass apart. Cutting it in half lengthwise, then across the middle, is often enough, but if you're back-packing a large animal out of the woods, it should be taken down into parts light enough to carry without necessitating back surgery down the road. Here we take a moose in fourths. The method is the same for all big game animals.

With a reciprocating saw, Dave starts splitting this moose from behind ➔ so he can line up on the spine. ⬇ Once the hip is split, he moves inside for a better angle; if you haven't taken the head off yet, now is the time. ⬇ Once split, Dave lines up between two vertebrae to halve the half for easier handling. ↘ Dave starts the cut below the sternum, so he has an easy route to finish the cut. (It also makes the four pieces about equal in weight.)

To take an animal down further in the field, see Five Easy Pieces, page 47. You may have to bone the meat out to get it home, but when possible keep the meat in recognizable chunks. You'll still want to know what cut you're eating, even if you did have to carry it out of the woods.

# Brisket & Flank

On larger animals like elk and moose--even water buffalo and our own bison--the meat lying over the rib cage, is well worth retrieving. It varies in thickness: from as much as 2 inches thick, it thins as it rises up the rib cage. On moose and elk it's a 4 to 5 pound cut perfect for braised slow-oven-cooking dishes and a St. Patty's Day corned brisket. On smaller animals brisket is thinner, more like flank steak and can be used as such; and while some is chewy, some is very tender. Here's John's Canada moose (below). Like hanging t-loins, remove brisket before aging so it doesn't dry out.

The brisket lies on the rib cage across the sternum--where the rib cage fuses to the sternum over the vital organs. Like the hanging tenderloin, it can dry out and be unusable if left on the carcass while it ages. So once your animal is skinned, it's a good idea to remove it. John's hand marks one end of the brisket. There's another piece of brisket on the other side.

Since the brisket runs under the shoulder, first cut through the connective tissue freeing the shoulder from the rib cage. Starting at the top of the brisket, lay your knife blade parallel to the ribs, pulling and slicing the brisket from the bone. (The process is a lot like skinning.) If you have help, ask them to hold the freed brisket out of your way.

Work your way down the rib cage, keeping your knife flat against the ribs. As you get down to the shoulder, have your helper rotate the shoulder away from the rib cage to make it easier to remove the brisket. Repeat for the chunk of brisket on the other side of the rib cage. Rinse, wrap, and age--or freeze the brisket.

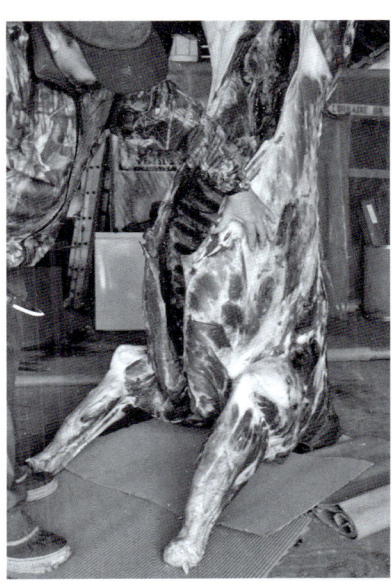
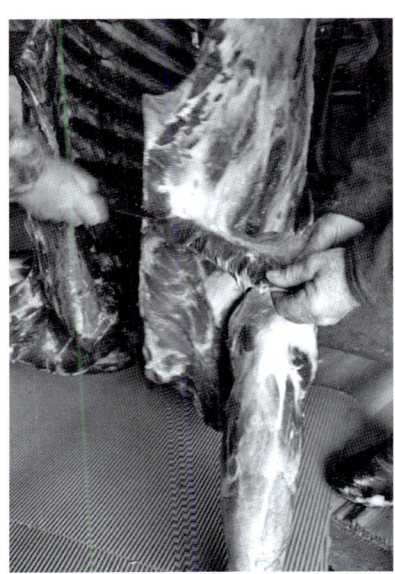
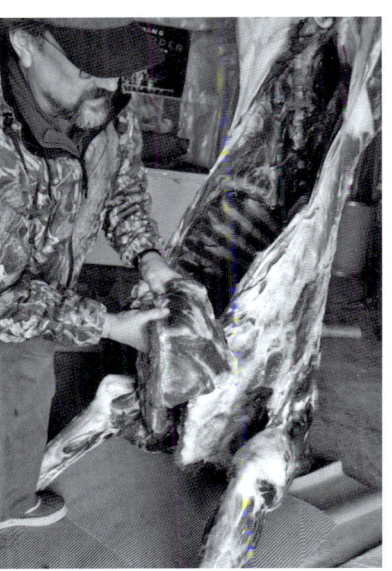

# Hanging Tenderloins

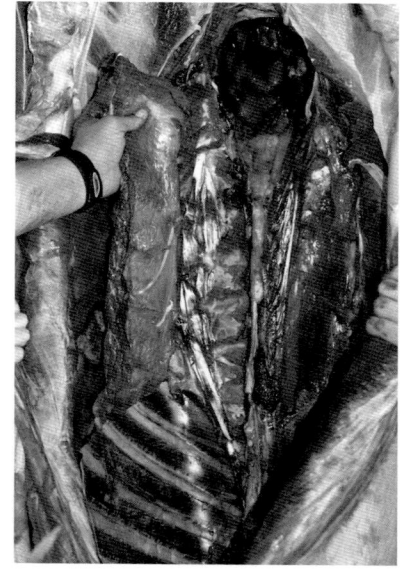

## The Tenderloin and Hanging Tenderloin

Before leaving this field section, it's important to do one more thing: remove the hanging tenderloins.

The tender cuts that lie both in and outside the carcass, on either side of the spine have a variety of names, some used interchangeably, and sometimes just consolidated into a lovingly said 'tenders.' I've heard the three most common names, tenderloin, backstraps, and filets used interchangeably for both tender cuts over the years in restaurants and butcher shops as well as home butchering books. Around campfires, the variations are endless, though my all-time favorites are overstraps and underloins.

To keep it simple, I've adopted the terms a rancher friend uses for his butchering: what sits on top of the spine, just under the skin, is the tenderloin. What lies inside the carcass is the hanging tenderloin. (He also points out that this latter piece is often referred to as the 'Butcher's Tenderloin' since it often disappears into the butcher's freezer.)

Obviously, the hanging tenderloin is the smaller of the two, the more tender of the two, and should be removed shortly after field dressing since it will dry out and shrink to the size and texture of a hockey puck if left to age with the rest of the carcass. Wait 24 hours, if you want. But no longer. It's easy to forget this luscious little piece of meat once you start unpacking your gear, and it can dry up to nothing very quickly.

← You can feel the hanging tenderloin; it sits on both sides of the spine, inside the carcass, from hip to 'waist.' To remove it, start on one side of the spine, freeing the hanging t-loin first from along the spine, then coming under it, keeping your knife edge hard up against the rib cage, as you move forward. (Just think of breasting a bird. Feel for the meat, then lift it off the bone structure.) Then repeat on the other side of the spine. (At left: one out, one to go.)

Rinse with clean cold water, trim, then pat dry, and place in a resealable plastic bag. You can still age the hanging t-loin in the refrigerator for a week if you want, as long as you leave the length intact. However, it's so tender, you can just dry, wrap and freeze it right away.

How do they compare? John recently shot a 200 pound mule deer buck: each trimmed and ready to cook tenderloin weighed 6 pounds; the hanging tenderloins weighed 1 pound each. The hanging t-loin is also more tender. I guess good things do come in smaller packages.

# Skinning

The epitome of a clean well-lighted place: Richard Mann, with son Bat, skin behind the family's hunting cabin. Starting at the inner thigh of one leg, split the skin from the field dressing cut up the inside of the thigh to the knee. (Anatomically, its the ankle, but since it's a foot off the ground, we all refer to it as the 'knee.') Cut through the skin at the knee; you'll toss the very lower leg, no need to skin it. With one hand, lift the skin and start slicing it free, pulling it gently but firmly away from the meat as you go. Skin the leg to the hip.

Bat helps by holding one leg to keep the carcass from spinning. With one leg skinned out, repeat for the second. Then, move to the back of the carcass grabbing the tail and begin freeing the skin from the back and sides, pulling down firmly but gently, while slicing through the membrane between skin and meat. About mid-back, set the knife down, and pull the skin down the back to the neck, rolling it gently. Slice through the connective tissue when needed.

Free the front legs as you did the hind legs; cut around the skin at the knee, then making a slit on the inner front leg from the dressing, cut to the knee. With one hand lift the skin from the muscle, and slice it free, pulling as you go. The skin is much easier to pull off an animal that's either very fresh, or been aged a week or so. When both shoulders are free, pull the entire hide down around the neck. Cut through the meat and connective tissue at the neck, then saw through the spine. When done, trim away the fat, and check for loose hair, dirt and crusty pieces.

# Moving Day

We're done in the garage, basement, or meat pole, wherever you hang game animals for skinning and aging. At our house that means we're moving into the kitchen where there's heat, running water and, best of all, a great collection of knives.

At right, are the latest in our collection: including two fillet, one boning, one 8-inch and one 10-inch Cimeter, and a skinning knife. All from Forschner. Notice the shapes: the two Cimeters in the middle are curved to make cutting steaks and roasts in one long swipe much easier; the skinning knife at top has a rounded drop-point to keep it from poking through the skin as well as a wider blade than the 2 fillet knives at bottom. (The fillet knives have two different flexes: the longer one, my favorite, has less flex than the shorter one, which is John's favorite.) We both like the synthetic pebbled finish of the Fibrox handles for a firm grip when our hands are wet. All keep an edge a long time, but are easy to sharpen back up with steel or stone.

What are your knives like? They don't have to be pretty, they just have to be functional, and I've found over the years that means different things to different people, like John and me with those fillet knives. His hands are beefier, though they're no longer; my dexterity more agile, his strength more durable. What feels good in my hand might not feel good in his or yours. So look at knives, imagine how you would use them, and slice the air. Be careful as you whip that Cimeter around that no salesperson is sneaking up behind you--but using knives is the best way to feel if the weight and balance is right for you.

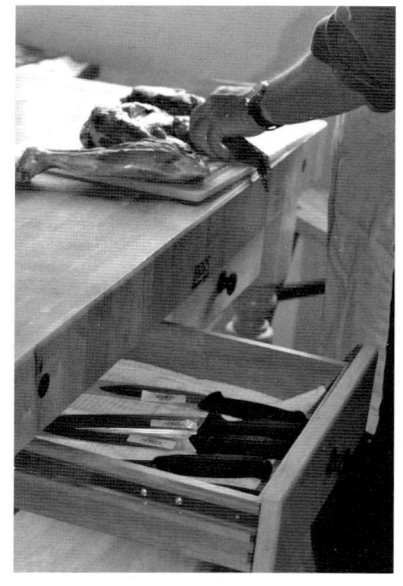

What knife is right for the job is easier. For bigger animals or bigger cuts, an 8 or 10-inch Cimeter makes neater long cuts without your working as hard. Fillet knives--with whatever whippiness you like--are essential for making the finer, smaller cuts. And boning knives are the butcher's workhorse. Can you imagine trimming bones with a 10-inch Cimeter? Or cutting an elk hind quarter with a pocket knife?

If you're just starting out, buy one boning knife (6 to 8-inches long) and one fillet knife (with some flex, but not as much as fish fillet knives that can bend over backwards while whistling the Twin Guitar Boogie). As you get into taking care of your own meat you will attract new knives as some hunters attract Mauser rifles---or English shotguns.

While John's out in the garage skinning the animal, I'm organizing the kitchen. Cutting boards, freezer paper, tape, pens, knives, and sharpening tools. I used to think sharp knives were dangerous, and John reinforced that our first year of marriage by slashing the back of his hand on the final swipe through a set of porcelain sharpening sticks. But over the years I've been converted. Yes, sharp knives cut quick, but dull knives are hard to control. They take more force for the same result and the more force you use, the more dangerous they are. Dull knives glance off of surfaces that a sharp knife would bite right into. Buy a set of good knives, then buy a stone and steel or, if you're no good at figuring angles, buy yourself an electric knife sharpener or sharpening kit, whichever fits your budget. And keep your knives sharp: it's easier to keep an edge than to rebuild one that's been totally dulled.

There's more moving on moving day, however, than this year's kill. We have three freezers at our house. And before we start putting any new meat in we have to organize what's left from last year. (It's not excess: it's a savings account.)

Each freezer has a role. The upright in the basement is for my cooking projects. Since I'm not the only one who likes to cook at our house, I stash cuts and species there that I want to have 3, 4, or 5 months down the road for recipe testing. (It also holds the raspberries, tomatoes, and cherries from our garden.)

There's also a chest freezer in the basement. It gets emptied each September so we can segregate all new meat in it, partly because it will take a few meals to know these animals better, but also because the older stuff needs to be eaten first. It's the most chaotic of the three, because on butchering day we strew fresh packages in, around, under, and through the already frozen ones--so they freeze faster. Mid-winter we go back and collect each animal into its own bag and bring order into chaos. But there's one corner that's permanent: we stash the exotics in this freezer so they last longer. Right now there are a few packages each of scimitar-horned oryx, bison, bighorn sheep, eland, and water buffalo.

What gets emptied out of the basement chest freezer goes upstairs to the chest freezer just off the kitchen. That's the one we're into day in and day out, lunch and dinner. Most of what's in there is less than a year old. But there are always a few packages that slip through the cracks, so when we organize this freezer, we arrange everything by date as well as cut. Over the years, we've collected a covey of tall, 12 to 14-inch square cardboard boxes that fit snugly in the freezer and form partitions: one each for steak, hamburger, roasts, stew, and upland birds: newest on bottom, oldest on top so they're eaten first.

Once the freezers are thawed, dried, and rearranged, we make a map of each one and tape it to the wall. Aside from making it easier for the cook to find one moose steak without pawing through all the antelope burger, fumbling, tumbling, and groping around is hard on paper. People tell me freezer paper causes freezer burn, but it's the abuse of freezer paper that does it. Single wrapping, and loosely wrapped, tumbled and frayed paper packages kept in upright freezers opened often--that's what causes freezer burn. Tightly double wrapped and stored in chest freezers, frozen meat keeps well long beyond any manufacturer's recommended freezer life.

Only have one freezer? The routine is the same: before you start adding new meat, empty out and re-organize the old. It's moving day. Better put some lively music on the radio. There's a lot to do!

# Gambrel To Table
## Custom Cutting

# The Basic Tools For Butchering

Last year I went shopping for a better butchering table. Like a lot of people, we had always used the kitchen counters (with cutting boards on top) to cut meat, but without under-cupboard lighting, that meant we were always facing away from the light. So I went to the local home supply store, thinking I could buy some sort of inexpensive counter top and screw some legs onto it, like a shooting bench. I asked, I looked, and nothing really fit my needs. Then I asked again, this time open to more options. The salesman looked at me like I was nuts and said, "We just do it on a piece of plywood in the garage."

Let's start with how many years he's used the same piece of plywood, the rough surface of the plywood, and the amount of bacterial growth on the plywood multiplied by those years. There's the inability to adequately clean such a rough surface, the chemicals and glue used to produce it, and the distinct possibility--no, probability--that some of that chemically treated, bacteria-laden surface has worked its way onto his fork. There are lots of people who worry about the bacteria on their cutting boards; who scrub them with hot soapy water or pour boiling water on them every time they use them. Is this man's wife one of those? Does she know the plywood out in the garage gets cleaned off with the garden hose after each animal? And nothing more? I don't want to even think about where that plywood gets stored between animals and between seasons. Not do I ever want to be invited to eat game at his house.

You need a clean, well-lighted place with a sturdy easy-to-clean table or counter, and a cutting board or two to protect the counter. (Some people place a tarp on the kitchen table, then cutting boards on top of the tarp.) Whatever you use, it should be a hard, relatively non-porous surface that can be cleaned well with hot soapy water. You'll need a 6 to 8-inch boning knife for the big cuts, a fillet knife for the trimming; knife sharpening equipment, freezer paper, tape, and a pen to date and label the cuts. It's not complicated. I can take a deer from gambrel to freezer, by myself in four hours or less. When John's helping, we each take a quarter and cut; or one makes the big cuts while the other trims and wraps. One person can do it; two's better; three makes the work go really fast. You'll also need a meat grinder if you eat venison burger. Processors grind the day's trimmings all at once. If you were careful with shot placement and field care, you don't want a year's supply of community burger in your freezer. It's just one of many reasons to butcher your own. We just upgraded a couple years ago to Cabela's 1/2 horsepower grinder (from the $100 kitchen store model that doesn't last as well as it used to, like everything else.) The new grinder has made grinding less of a chore, and it's much quieter and faster.

Always keep a bowl of warm water handy, both for dampening a paper towel and warming your hands. The colder the meat is, the easier it is to cut cleanly (something short of frozen solid is best) but the harder it is on your hands. They get cold, and then they start to hurt. (Or is that just a sign the hunting population in our house is getting older?) Plus animal hair is sticky and if you wipe it on your apron or jeans it is hard to get off; but it floats right off in water.

Always double wrap your meat with at least 2 layers of good freezer paper, and press out as much air as possible as you wrap and tape. For special meat you want to keep longer than one year, wrap first with plastic wrap, then double wrap with freezer paper. Once frozen, collect all those long-storage packages into a paper grocery bag or box, whatever will fit, and stow it in one corner of the freezer. You'll know where to find it, but it won't get tumbled and pawed through when you're looking for more everyday meat. It will keep longer that way.

How much meat do you wrap in each package? Depends on the size and appetites of your family. For two-person households like ours, a 1-pound package of burger or steak makes a meal. Perhaps you have teens? Or entertain a lot? Wrap whatever you'll eat in one meal, whether it's one, two, or five pounds at a time.

One more thing. People laugh when we first tell them this, but after we explain they start doing it themselves. We name all of our game animals. We dubbed John's last moose Double Hung because we first saw him with another bull, heads together, their antlers overlapping. The big whitetail I took with Scott Sundheim we named Scoot, Scott's nickname. We name them because we both hunt, both take several game animals a year, sometimes on the same day, and if one of them is bad, we want to be able to remove the bad apple from the barrel. If they're just marked with the date, or month and year, it's harder. Plus, names stick in your head. And if you're suspicious of an animal, like the mule deer buck I shot many years ago during the rut, it's easier to keep an eye on that meat: I named that mule deer Randy. And he was randy. A month after we'd put him in the freezer, we were digging him back out and grinding him into sausage. Without individual, distinctive labeling, we would have been accidently eating Randy for months.

There's another advantage of butchering your own meat: instead of generically marked 'steak' you can label specifically--rump steak, for instance, because rump is more tender than shoulder, and loin is more tender than rump. You wouldn't buy a piece of beef at the grocery store that was just labeled 'steak.' You wouldn't know how to cook it. (And know what it was worth at checkout.) Why should that be any different with your wild game? It helps the cook to know what's in that little white package. Perhaps the game cook in your family would even try something besides the old standby, chile, if he/she knew, beforehand, how good the meat would taste at the table.

If there's a name right there on the white paper, you remember that day, but you also remember what that animal tasted like the last time you cooked it. You know how tender or tough, how large or small the steaks are on that particular animal. You can segregate the iffy ones, and maybe try new recipes with animals you know are tasty and tender. That all helps the cook, and makes meal time less stressful.

# The Choices: Parting It Out

We start by separating the 5 major parts from the carcass: the 2 front quarters, the 2 hind quarters, and the tenders, both tenderloins and hanging tenderloins. Then it's time to decide what cuts you like best, and therefore, what specific smaller parts to cut the five big parts into. If you still have meat in the freezer, go see what lasted so long. You probably don't want too much of that. What did you run out of first? Cut more of those. Are you thinking you should simplify your life and make more comfort food? I can't think of anything more comfortable than pot roast and slow cooker roasts. Meat, gravy, and mashed potatoes! Take a minute. Eat some chocolate chip cookies. If you're not the one who does most of the cooking, talk to the cook. Talk to the eaters. Then make a plan. There's no rule that says you have to cut steaks on the upper hind quarter. No rule that says you have to cut steaks at all. But in most houses that would be like not buying donuts for Saturday morning garage sales. Just be sure what you do cut is what you want.

If you're lucky enough to take several game animals over the season, you can let each animal specialize: that fat young forkhorn into all steaks; all pot roasts off that rangy, down-in-the-mouth trophy buck or bull. (There's also no rule that says you can't wrap and freeze quarters until you know exactly how you want to cut them. We've wrapped quarters many times, then thawed, cut, and re-frozen them. As long as you keep the meat icy cold--and not thaw them to room temperature--it won't hurt a thing.) Do the T & T Test before you make a final decision. What's most tender should be saved for the Tender End sections of this book--quick-grilled or pan-roasted steaks, and dry roasted rumps and loins. What's tougher should be assigned to the Tough End sections--long, moist cooking pot roasts, and cover & cook recipes. What's tougher yet goes into the Tough & Tougher section--burger and, when gamy, into heavily spiced dishes and sausage.

Mark your packages accordingly, using our naming method, or assigning a grade: from 5 stars to none, or A to F. (Keep it simple: I've been known to name gamy animals after really bad movie stars or nice people who just happen to have appropriate names, like Randy.) Now let's get to work. And the first thing to do is the T & T Test.

## Taste & Tenderness Test

If the animal looks healthy and fat, test a shoulder steak; if that's tender, you have a totally tender animal. If the shoulder steak is tough, test a hind quarter steak. Chances are, unless all you shoot is trophy, rutting, ancient animals, the shoulder will be a little chewy but readily marinatable and the rump will be tender enough for quick-grilling. If you're not getting that at least most of the time, you need to re-evaluate your field care, hanging, and aging procedures.

To test a shoulder steak: Lightly oil a cast iron fry pan, and turn it onto medium-high heat. When the oil starts to sizzle, toss a steak onto the pan. Let it cook until blood appears on the top, then turn and cook half again as long. Sprinkle with a bit of salt and pepper and taste it. (Where do you cut it? Check out custom cutting the front quarter, page 55.)

You may want to cook only a small part of the steak, or rub a little garlic butter over it. Two or three cloves, minced and stirred into a tablespoon of softened butter, then rubbed or spread on the steak as it finishes cooking, does the job.

## Sinew

I've been in hunting camps where the cutters stripped each muscle off the carcass, then ruthlessly stripped all the sinew off the muscle, even the totally transparent silver skin. It's one way to cut, but it takes more time and energy and, unless you're cutting a stunk-in-the-rut mule deer, elk or caribou, if you can see through the connective tissue it's not going to be a problem for the cook--or the eater. And honestly, a stunk-in-the-rut animal is best left for the sausage maker. Taking the thick, tough sinew helps, but taking the silver skin--especially on animals that weren't rutty in the first place--is nothing more than a lot of extra work. The worst part is that these pieces of meat are then thrown into a communal pile--tender with tough--of amorphous chunks that you now can't analyze and are stuck with having to cook all of it long and moist. As much game as we eat, I want quick at least some nights, and I want a little variety from week to week in what gets plopped down on my plate.

# The Five Easy Pieces

Ready? Knives sharp? Freezer paper, masking or freezer tape, permanent markers, and a little Beach Boy music on the stereo round out the bare necessities.

Start by dividing the carcass into its five major parts: front quarters, hind quarters, and the tenders. Here the hind quarters come off first. The hind quarter is connected to the carcass at the hip socket, a ball and socket joint. It's a very strong connection, just because of it's shape, and the ligaments make it stronger yet. (It's why you rarely hear of athletes dislocating hips. Shoulders and knees, yes. But hips, rarely.) On the other hand, if you're fresh and wide awake, a little cutting and lifting will sever the ligaments and the ball will pop out of the socket easily. (It's the main reason we start with the hip joint.) Here's how we do it.

## Separating The Hind Quarters

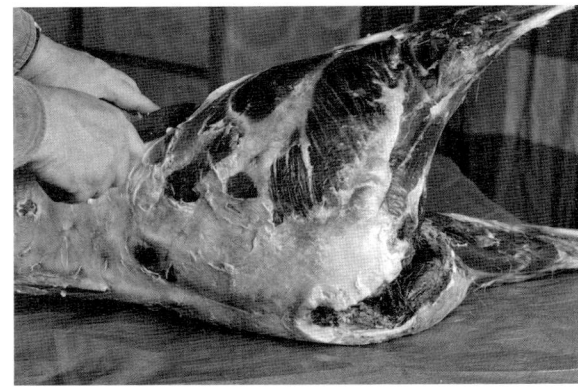

1. The ribs end inches in front of the thigh, so there is nothing to stop you from cutting right down to the spine. Set your knife in front of the thigh, and cut straight down until you hit bone.

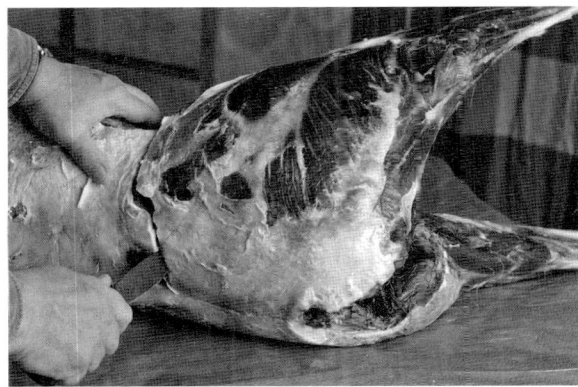

2. When you hit the spine, angle the knife along the top edge of the hip bone. To the left is the tenderloin; to the right, the rump roast. Even if you tried you could not cut the tenderloin from withers to tail bone: the crest of the hip bone flares out just left of the knife, and would stop you cold.

5 easy pieces ◇ hind quarter

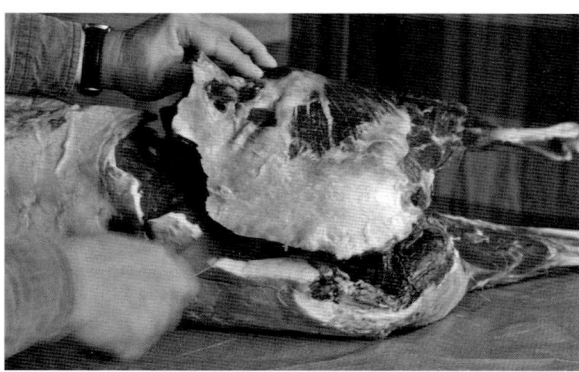

3. Line your knife up parallel to the spine and slice into the fat and meat at the top of the rump. Once that first cut is made through the fat and meat, cut deeper.

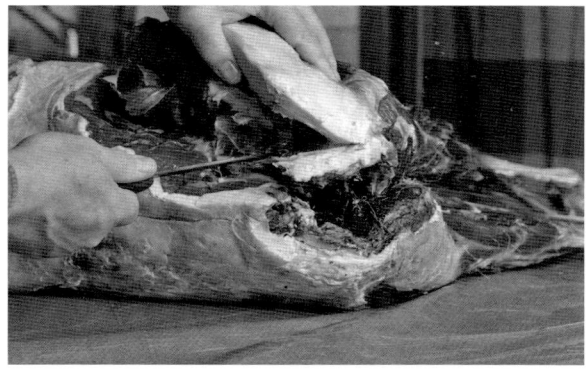

4. Lift that edge and cut toward the hip joint, keeping your knife as close to the hip bone as possible. (It's like a flat plate hanging down from the spine; and the thigh bone plugs into it.) Like breasting a bird; keep your knife blade flat to the bone/plate.

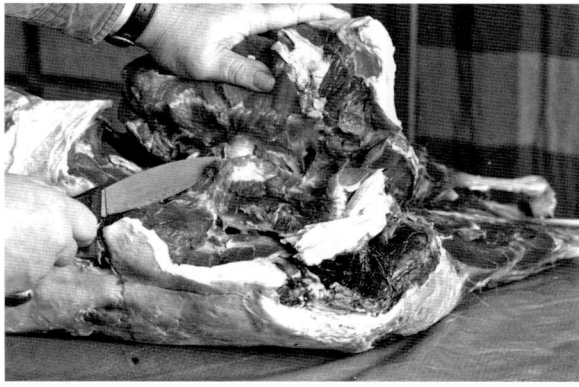

5. The hip joint is a sturdy ball and socket construction: the ball is the top of the thigh bone (see the point of the knife) and fits into the socket (or pocket) that's part of that 'hanging plate.' Cut through the meat and ligaments and you weaken and expose that joint.

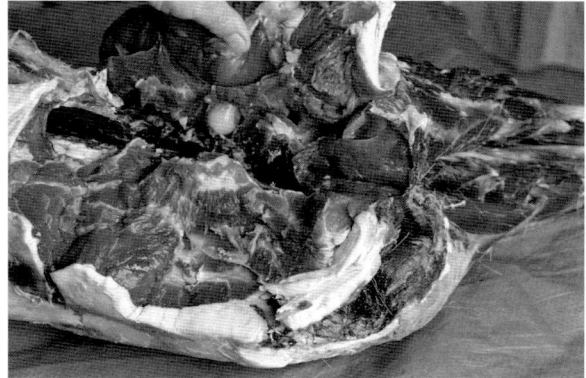

6. Lift the hind quarter and cut through the ligaments holding the ball in place. Then grasp the lower leg and lift, exposing the last of the meat holding the hind quarter to the carcass on the inside of the leg. Slice through that meat. Set the first hind quarter aside, and repeat.

Slice Of The Wild

# Separating The Tenderloin

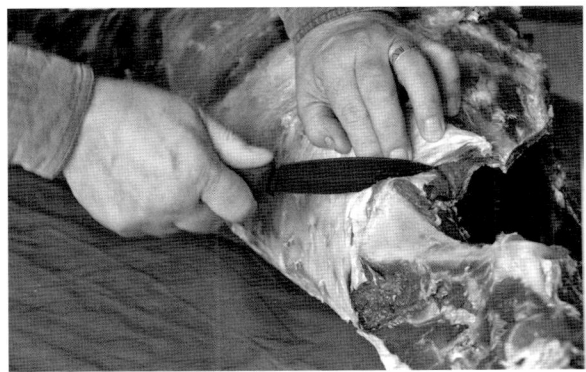

7. To remove the tenderloin: starting at the front of the hip bone, which you already exposed when removing the hind quarter, cut straight down to the spine.

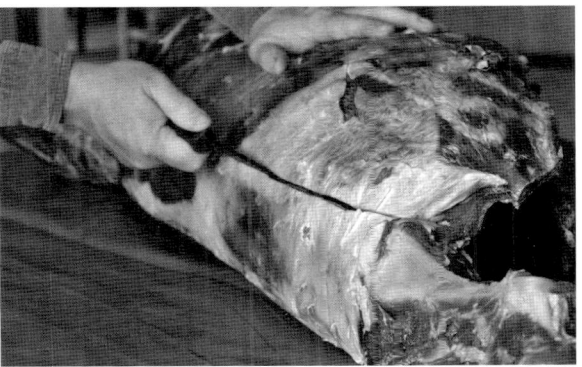

8. The tenderloin is a triangle, thickest at the spine and tapering down along the rib cage. Feel for where the loin peters out, then score the meat along that edge of the rib cage.

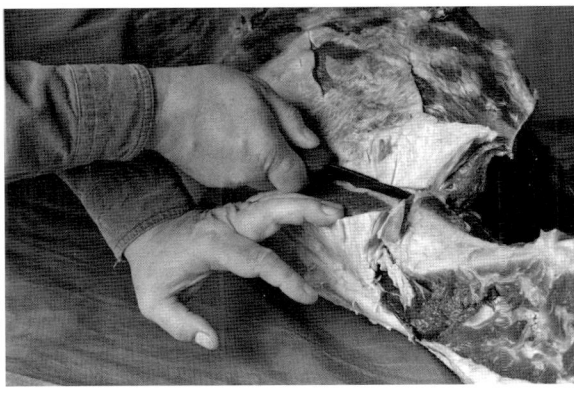

9. Starting at the score line, free the loin from the rib cage, keeping your knife parallel to the ribs so you don't lose any meat. There are no bones or tough ligaments to interfere, so pretend it's a pheasant breast and fillet it cleanly off the bone.

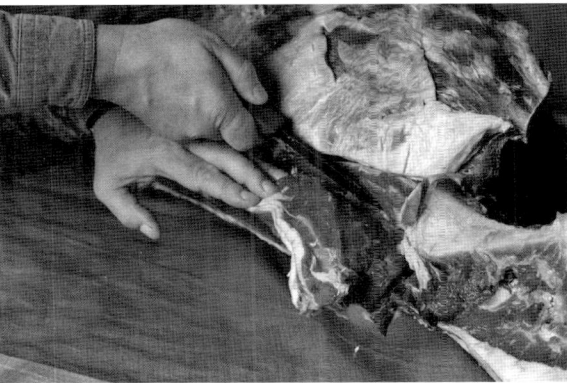

10. Alternate from the rib side to the spine side of the tenderloin, slicing the meat from the bone and lifting the free end out of your way as you move from the hip end to the shoulder blade. (Or the withers, if you're a horse person.)

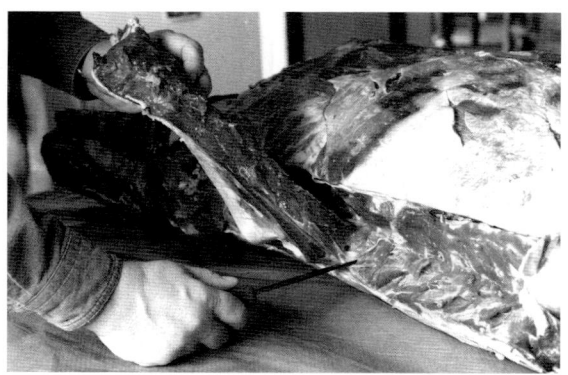

11. Lift and cut as you move toward the shoulder. If there are two more hands available, one person can cut while the other lifts. On larger animals like moose and elk, each tenderloin can weigh several pounds.

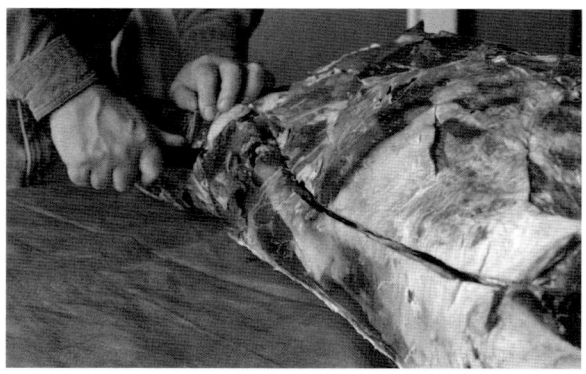

12. At the top of the shoulder joint, cut the tenderloin off at a 90° angle--across the grain. Trim, rinse, wrap, and let the loins age in the refrigerator for several days. They, too, improve with aging. Repeat for the other side.

## The Tenders

→ Once the tenderloin is free, lay it out on a cutting board; trim away any fat, sinew, bloodshot and crusty spots, until you have a fresh, neat-looking cut of meat. Depending on the size of your family, and the size of the animal this tenderloin belongs to, wrap it whole, or cut the length in half or thirds. If you intend to cut medallions (left foreground, at right) wait until you're ready to cook them. Larger chunks of meat fare better in the freezer.

Do the same for the second tenderloin, and the hanging tenderloins if you haven't removed them yet. (See page 38.) On deer-sized animals, the two pieces of hanging tenderloin won't be much more than a pound of meat together, but an elk or moose hanging tender is large enough to cut into sections and medallions.

I've seen people choose cover & cook recipes for tenders, but that's usually overkill. Choose a Tender End recipe, and remember that the hanging t-loin is usually more tender than the t-loin, and both are more tender toward the rump than the shoulder, relatively speaking.

# Separating The Front Quarters

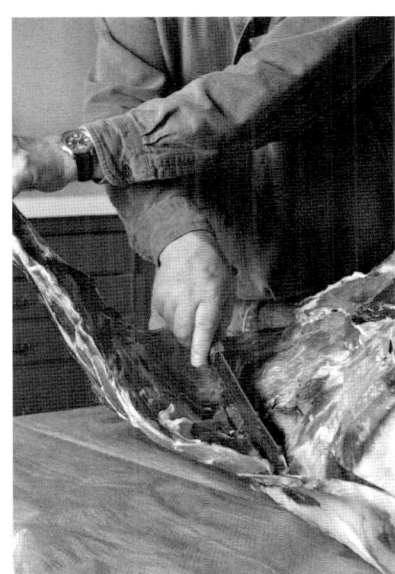

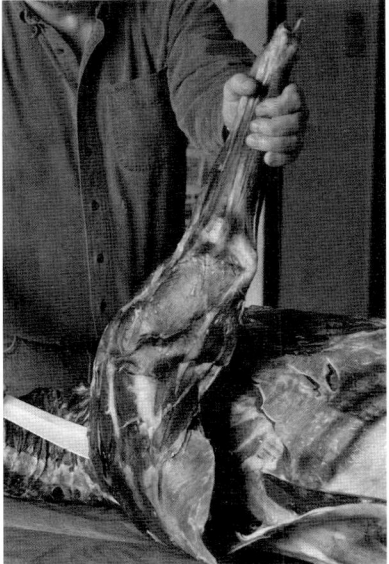

## Shoulder Structure

Removing a front quarter is much easier than a hind quarter. Unlike the hip, the shoulder is a friction joint: the upper arm bone (humerus) collar bone (clavicle), and shoulder blade (scapula) fit together rather than lock into each other--with ligaments the only thing holding them in place. Once you rotate the shoulder away from the rib cage, those ligaments will be right under your knife.

↖ Start by lifting the shoulder away from the rib cage.
↑ Lay the knife parallel to the rib cage and slice through the connective tissue.
↗ Keep pulling the shoulder away from the rib cage, as you slice, keeping one side of the knife blade flat to the ribs to collect as much shoulder meat as possible.
← Lift and slice, until you reach the spine, then make one clean slice at the spine to free the shoulder. (If you have a 10-inch boning knife, this is a good place to use it.) At that point, there will only be a thin layer of meat left to cut through. Repeat for the second shoulder.

# Cutting The Hind Quarters

*custom cutting*

1 & 2. Have you made your plan? Put a hind quarter on the cutting board. With your fingers, feel for the top of the thigh bone (femur); this is the ball of the ball/socket hip joint. Then cut straight across the top of the thigh meat at the top of the ball. This is a tender piece of meat, usually, and will make a nice, small roast, or you can cut it into bite-sized chunks. We label those 'tender chunks' and use them for stir-fries, or a quick-cooking soup, chili, or stew.

◇

*hind quarter*

 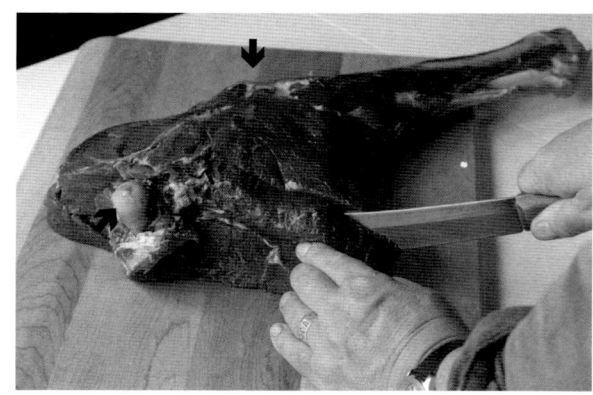

3. Now that the thigh bone is exposed, make one more cut below the ball, as straight as you can 90 degrees on both sides of the femur. This makes for a neat cut on your first steak or the top of a roast, and the meat cut away for trim qualifies for 'tender chunk' status, as above.

4. The femur runs from the ball to the knee (note arrows). Starting at the femur, cut the steaks at a 90° angle. The back of the thigh has the larger chunk of meat: on an average-sized whitetail buck, you can cut four 3/4 or 1-inch thick steaks here.

Slice Of The Wild

5. Free the steaks from the femur by cutting as close as you can along the length of the bone.

6. Set the steaks aside as you free them. How was your T & T Test? If this is an average animal, these high hind quarter steaks will work for quick grilling and pan roasting recipes starting on page 60.

## Other People, Other Ways

A lot of people cut the meat from the bone first, then cut the steaks, even when they're already in the kitchen. We prefer cutting bone-in for two reasons: it's easier to keep the meat anchored and cut neater, more uniform steaks (so the entire steak is the same thickness from end to end and will cook evenly); if you're a novice butcher, it's also easier to keep track of the grain of the meat when it's still on the bone. (If you've ever had to bone an animal out in the field, you know how hard it can get just to identify what quarter you're dealing with once you get it home for butchering, much less what end of the cut it is. And the end counts: lower and forward are always tougher than high and rear.)

Muscles attach at the ends of long bones, like the femur and humerus, and grain runs the direction of the length. So if you want to cut across grain, you set your knife at a 90° angle to the bone and cut as if you were going to cut through it--but don't. Europeans often cut the meat with the grain, and when we make muscle meat jerky, we sometimes cut with the grain, because it is chewier that way. Obviously though, chewier is not a good thing when it comes to steaks and roasts.

7. It's easier for the cook to time steaks when they're an even thickness from one end to the other. The easiest way to do that is to cut while the meat is somewhat frozen, as we did with those stacked above. Of course in Montana, in November, this is a natural state of affairs.

custom cutting ◇ hind quarter

8. Once you've freed the steaks from the back of the thigh, turn the hind quarter around, and do the same for the front. This is a slightly smaller chunk of meat, so usually yields one less steak than the back of the thigh.

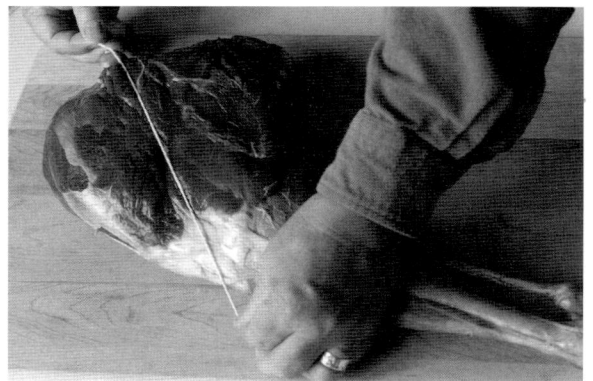

9. If roasts are more popular at your house, cut two big roasts from the hind quarter instead. (Or cut steaks from one, and roasts from the other. The string marks the position of the femur, or thigh bone.

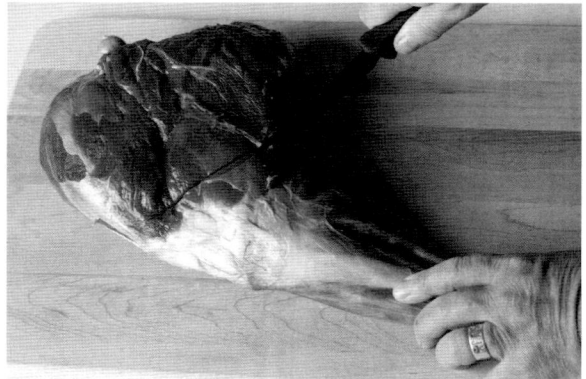

10. Cut across the femur, above the knee. Above the knife is more tender; below less. Cut along the length of the femur, freeing the smaller of the two rump roasts. Trim away any fat that sits between the femur and the thigh meat. If you need to, tie the roast, as we will with the shoulder blade roast later.

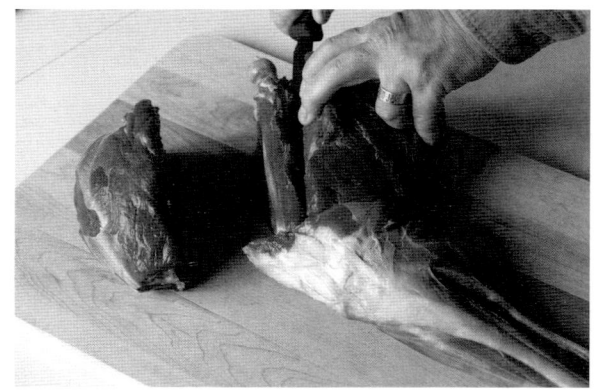

11. Cut along the other side of the femur for the second roast. You could keep the femur in the roast, by separating it from the lower leg at the knee. (Hyper-extend the knee and cut through the connective tissue and ligaments. It's fairly easy.) This makes a very large roast, ideal if you're feeding a big group. Or just tie the two roasts together. All are great for dry roasting, starting on page 98.

54 Slice Of The Wild

# Cutting The Front Quarters

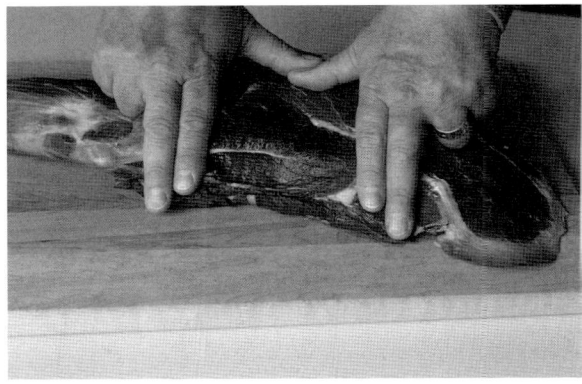

12. There are three to four 3/4 or 1-inch steaks to be taken from the shoulder on deer-sized animals, in the soft muscle area where the shoulder blade meets the upper leg bone (humerus).

14. Then free the steaks by cutting along one side of the length of the bone, as you did for the hindquarter.

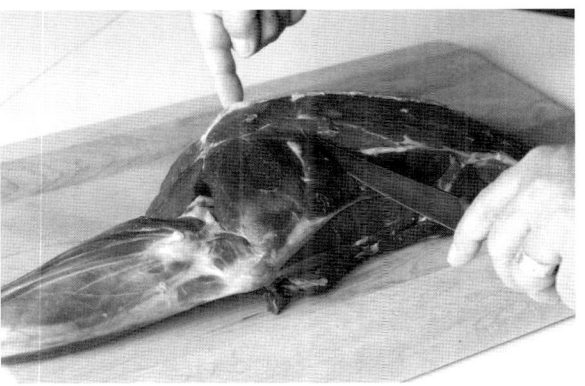

13. Start at the middle of this area; pointing your knife directly at the joint, slice down for each steak.

## To Steak Or Not To Steak

Steaks are always the first thing to disappear from our freezer these days. So we're always looking for more places to take a steak or two. This area of the shoulder is a good one on young tender animals.

Have you done the T & T Test? If your test shoulder steak was tender, these shoulder steaks will as good as rump steaks quick-grilled or pan-roasted. If the test steak was tougher than you can fix with an overnight marinade, just bone out the shoulder steak meat and run it though the grinder. Hamburgers, and ground venison in general, are second only to steaks in popularity at our house, and probably number one in others. Starting on page 146, there's chili, spaghetti and meatballs, tortilla pie, cheeseburgers, brats . . .

custom cutting ◆ front quarter

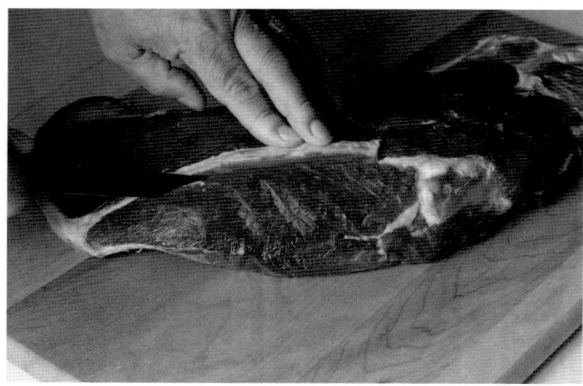

15. The shoulder blade is essentially a flat paddle with a ridge running down the middle (under John's finger). Starting at the ridge, bone out each side of the ridge as if it was a pheasant breast.

16. Cut the shoulder blade meat off neatly at one end.

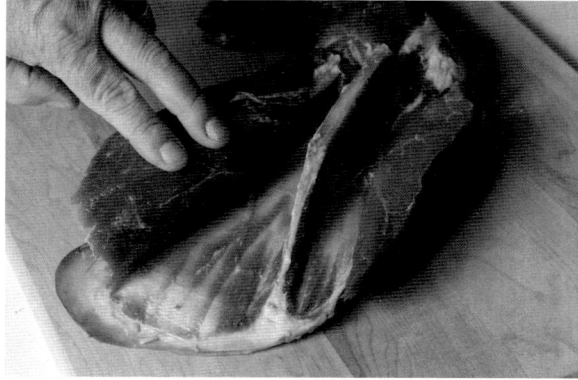

17. Now, bone out the other side of the ridge. Keep as much meat for the rolled roast as possible; you'll place them back to back, thin end of one lined up with the fat end of the other, for even cooking and slicing.

18. This side of the shoulder blade produces two fairly large chunks of meat. Now flip the shoulder blade over. Most deer-sized animals don't have much meat there, but larger animals will. Small pieces get added to the burger pile; larger ones can be folded into the rolled roasts.

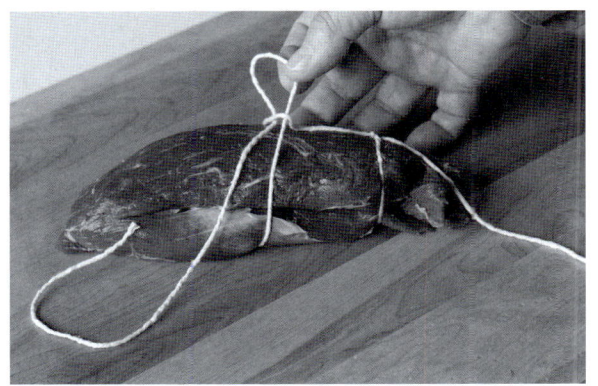
← You can add all the shoulder blade meat to the burger/sausage pile if that's what your family likes best, but we like pot roasts, and a tied deer shoulder makes a nice one-pot meal for two to four people. On larger deer, elk, and moose, it's big enough to feed 6 to 8. Check out the slow cook, and cover & cook recipes for these roasts starting on page 127.

To tie the roast: Set the two pieces of meat back to back, but flip them fat end to thin end. Cut an 18-inch length of cotton string, then make a simple knot leaving a 5 or 6-inch tag end. Run the long end down the length of the roast, looping it around the roast and string 2 to 3 times. Anchor it by tying to the tag end.

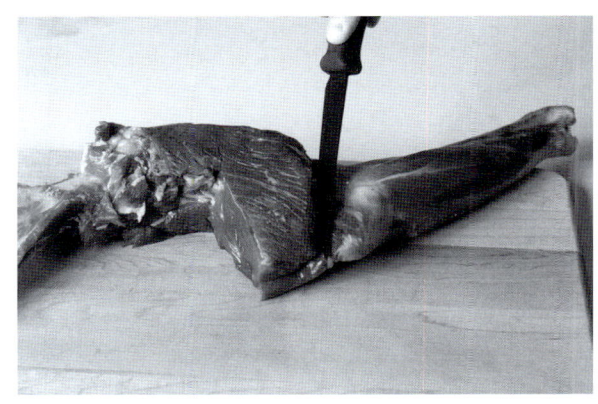
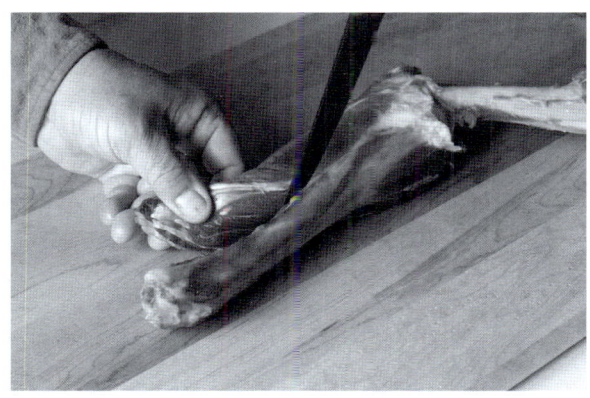

↑With the shoulder steaks and shoulder blade meat gone, the rest is burger (left of the knife), and stew meat (right of the knife). What makes the difference? The stew meat has lots of connective tissue per pound of usable meat and even if you use a very powerful grinder, the sinew slows you down. (It totally strangles lesser machines.) Plus, if you have a gamy animal, the connective tissue is one of the places where those flavors concentrate. It's easier to just chop them into a highly spiced chili or stew. →To remove the stew meat, stab the point of the knife between the bone and the muscle. Then slide the knife down and around the bone to free the meat. Do the same for the hind quarter's lower legs.

Slice Of The Wild

## Tips & Tactics:
### How Much Do You Get?

Since we live on game meat year round, John and I always try to get at least four deer-sized animals a year for the freezer. More is better. With our butchering methods, we can count on putting about 30% of the dressed weight of the animal into the freezer as boned meat. Take this fall, for instance: the forkhorn mule deer buck I shot probably weighed 100 pounds on the hoof, 30% less once field dressed, and yielded about 25 pounds of boned steak, roasts, and burger meat. (He had a little damage to his shoulder blade, so we lost 1 to 2 pounds there.)

The big muley buck John shot in Wyoming probably weighed 180 pounds field dressed; he yielded close to 60 pounds of boned meat. The big antelope buck John took was noticeably bigger than any antelope we'd taken before and dwarfed my doe. She yielded about 5 pounds more boned meat than my forkhorn mule deer, but John's gargantuan antelope buck yielded almost 10 pounds more than her.

John got lucky and took a bull elk this year. Percentage-wise, mature elk lose more weight than deer to field dressing, but he'll still yield 150 pounds of meat. This year the bird hunting will be strictly for fun.

## What's Left?

Several years ago, I decided I would learn to reload my own rifle ammo so John wouldn't have to do it. So he walked me through it several times, and I made out a cheat-sheet with all the steps, and drawings of what tools went with what step so I could one day solo at the reloading bench. But before that day came, a friend who needed to do a little reloading himself dropped by.

John got us both started, getting out all the tools from all their hidey-holes in his reloading shop, and he went off to do something else. Half an hour went by and Tommy and I worked diligently, but not very fast. When John came back we had loaded 3 or 4 cartridges, between us, in the same time he could have loaded a box of 50. He banished me from the reloading room. Forever. Turned out I was a bit over-obsessive about getting the powder charge exactly right. But that same tendency makes me the perfect one to wield the fillet knife on butchering days because once you've cut off all the obvious stuff, there are still several pounds of good meat on that carcass.

If you're keeping ribs, rather than trimming them, you need to cut them into packageable lengths; if not, that meat between the ribs should be gleaned for the burger pile. But after that, it's just a matter of picking up the little pieces that get left behind in butchering. But not all of it is burger. The leftovers from rump steaks and tenderloins, for instance may not be big enough for a steak, but are still tender. At our house, they become Tender Chunks, which then get sorted according to size and wrapped in 1-pound packages. (Large chunks with large; small with small so they'll cook at the same rate.) On most deer-sized animals we'll get 4 or 5 pounds of tender chunks. They are perfect for stir-fries, kabobs, and really quick-cooking soups and stews. Who doesn't need a few of those recipes? (To convert stew and soup recipes from true stew meat to Tender Chunks, just reduce the cooking time. Thirty minutes should be perfect.) So cut, wrap, and trim until the bones start to squeak, because what's next is the cooking. You'll want lots of meat for that.

# The Tender End
## Steaks and Medallions

# Grilled Venison Steaks with Garlic Butter
Serves 2-4

This recipe is as simple as a recipe gets. Start with a grilled steak on a hot summer afternoon. Then make up a bit of garlic butter and slather it on the steaks just before they come off the grill. By the time the steak platter arrives at the table, it will be awash in a rich butter sauce. Did you thaw enough venison for seconds?

## Ingredients
1 pound venison steaks
2 tablespoons butter, softened
4-6 cloves garlic, minced

## Cooking
1. Preheat the grill to medium-high heat. In a small bowl, combine the butter and minced garlic. Set aside.
2. Brush the steaks lightly with oil so they won't stick to the cooking surface. Place on the grill and close the lid.
3. Cook until blood appears on the top of the steaks, then turn, and cook about half again as long. A 3/4-inch thick steak will take about 7-10 minutes, total for both sides, for medium rare.
4. Just before you take the steaks off the grill, brush them with the garlic butter (or spread it on with a table knife) and then transfer them to a heated platter. Serve hot, with more garlic butter at the table.

## Tips & Tactics: Steaks from Tenders

This section isn't only for traditional steaks cut from traditional places. You can also create steaks--or medallions--by slicing tenderloins and hanging tenderloins across the grain, about 3/4-inch thick. They can then be used in any of these steak recipes, though if you choose to use one with a marinade, limit it to 2-4 hours because tenderloins and hanging tenderloins are almost always tender.

Over the years I've heard tenderloin and backstrap used interchangeably for these two cuts, as well as the terms 'tenders'--for both cuts--and 'overloins' for the upper cut, and on and on. Even professional meat cutters don't agree on terminology. Regionally, even block to block, it changes.

In our kitchen, and in this book, I use the easiest and most descriptive terminology I've heard so far--tenderloin and hanging tenderloin--offered by a Nevada beef rancher when I pointed at the tenderloin of the moose John had just killed and asked: What do you call that? The tenderloin is the upper piece; the hanging tenderloin is inside the body cavity hanging from the rib cage. And my Nevada friend points out that the hanging tenderloin is also called the 'butcher's' tenderloin among his neighbors, because when they take their steers to be butchered, it's the cut that often doesn't come back.

For photos and details, check out the butchering section of this book.

# Grilled Venison Steaks with Herbed Butter

Serves 2-4

Is it summer? Are there fresh herbs available? Then let's take the garlic butter up a step or two in flavor. Here is the same basic recipe, but with four variations in flavor. Herbed butters can be prepared ahead of time and stored up to 2 months in the freezer, but they're always better fresh.

## Ingredients
1 pound venison steaks
2 tablespoons herbed butter of your choice

## Cooking
1. Preheat the grill to medium-high heat. Brush the steaks lightly with oil so they won't stick to the cooking surface. Place on the grill and close the lid.
2. Cook until blood appears on the top of the steaks, then turn, and cook about half again as long. A 3/4-inch thick steak will take about 7-10 minutes, total for both sides, for medium rare.
3. Just before you take the steaks off the grill, brush them with the herbed butter of your choice (or spread it on with a table knife) and then transfer them to a heated platter. Serve hot, with more herbed butter at the table.

## Wild Sides: More Herbed Butters

Start with softened butter, and then mix, double wrap in plastic wrap, and chill. To store more than a day or two, double wrap and drop in a plastic freezer bag. Use a mini-chopper for the rest of the ingredients, if you want; but mince the herbs by hand and fold them in last.

Ritzy Tex-Mex: 1/2 cup butter, 1 tablespoon finely diced red onion, 2 teaspoons minced garlic, and 1/4 cup chopped fresh cilantro.

Smoky Tex-Mex: 1/2 cup butter, 1 tablespoon minced sun dried tomato, 2 tablespoons minced garlic, and 1 teaspoon smoked Chipotle Tabasco sauce.

Tuscan: 1/2 cup butter, 2 tablespoons minced shallots, 2 tablespoons minced garlic, and 1/4 cup chopped fresh oregano.

Traditional Herbed Butter: 1/2 cup butter, 1 tablespoon freshly squeezed lemon juice, 1 tablespoon chopped shallots, 1/2 teaspoon salt, and 1/4 teaspoon coarse black pepper.

# Dr. Pepper's Marinated Steaks
Serves 2-4

This may be one of the easiest marinades in the world, with a slightly sweet, slightly tangy flavor. If you haven't used black bean sauce in your cooking yet, you'll find it in a short, squat jar in the Asian section of the grocery store.

## Ingredients
1 cup Dr. Pepper
1 tablespoon black bean sauce
1/2 teaspoon cayenne pepper
1 pound venison steaks

## Preparation
1. Combine the Dr. Pepper, black bean sauce, and cayenne pepper in a resealable plastic bag.
2. Trim and dry the steaks, and add to the marinade. Seal, and let marinate 24 to 48 hours in the refrigerator.

## Cooking
1. Preheat the grill to medium-high heat. Let the steaks come to room temperature. Remove from the marinade, but don't dry or rinse the marinade off. That way, they don't stick to the cooking surface. Place on the grill and close the lid.
2. Cook until blood appears on the top of the steaks, then turn, and cook about half again as long. A 3/4-inch thick steak will take about 7-10 minutes, total for both sides, for medium rare.
3. Transfer to a heated platter. Serve hot, with Grilled Chiles Rellenos.

# Wild Sides: Grilled Chiles Rellenos
Serves 4

This is as close as I've ever come to the old-world traditional chiles rellenos flavor and texture, without all the work.

## Ingredients
2 Anaheim chiles
4 ounces Monterey Jack cheese, sliced thick
1 egg white, beaten until frothy

## Cooking
1. Preheat the grill to medium-high heat. Fold a doubled piece of aluminum foil up at the sides and ends to make a boat just big enough for the chiles to lie in a single layer without touching. Slice the chiles in half, lengthwise, remove the seeds and spine, and lay them cut-side up in the boat.
2. Lay a slice of cheese down the length of the chiles, then pour the frothy egg white over them, catching as much of the egg white in the halved chile as you can.
3. Place the boat on the grill, and cook until the egg white begins to brown, about 20 minutes. Slide the boat onto a serving plate, and carefully remove each piece with a spoon. Serve hot.

# The Four Ingredient Wonder
Serves 2-4

Traditionally, classically, marinades consist of acid to tenderize, oil to moisten and some seasoning to flavor the meat. Since this 'marinade' has no acid, it's more of a flavor and moisture enhancer. But it does a great job at that, and is almost as simple as opening a bottle of salad dressing--and, I think, better flavored.

## Ingredients
1/4 cup oil
3 cloves garlic, minced
1 teaspoon salt
1/2 teaspoon coarse ground black pepper
1 pound venison steaks

## Preparation
1. Combine the oil, garlic, salt, and pepper in a resealable plastic bag.
2. Trim the steak and dry with paper towels. Add to the marinade and let marinate 3 to 24 hours in the refrigerator.

## Cooking
1. Preheat the grill to medium-high heat. Let the steaks come to room temperature. Remove from the marinade, but don't dry or rinse the marinade off. That way, they won't stick to the cooking surface. Place on the grill and close the lid
2. Cook until blood appears on the top of the steaks, then turn, and cook about half again as long. A 3/4-inch thick steak will take about 7-10 minutes, total for both sides for medium rare.
3. Transfer to a heated platter. Serve hot.

****For a little more flavor, add 1 to 2 tablespoons of fresh minced oregano (or 1 to 2 teaspoons dried) to the marinade.

## Tips & Tactics: Re-Using Marinades

Save your marinades. They can be re-used for up to 5 days. But they can't be re-used as an after-cooking dip or sauce unless you re-heat them. Bring the marinade to a boil then simmer for 4 minutes. That will kill any bugs the raw meat may have left behind. Be safe, not sick.

## Wild Sides: Grilled Sweet Bells
Serves 2-4

Red bell peppers are just that old standby green bell pepper allowed to ripen a bit longer on the vine, which makes them much sweeter.

### Ingredients
1 red bell pepper
1 cup fresh salsa
4 ounces grated Monterey Jack cheese

### Cooking
1. Preheat the grill to medium-high heat. Cut the pepper in half lengthwise, then again lengthwise through the spine forming a cup to hold the filling.
2. Divide the salsa among the four pieces of pepper, then top with the cheese. Grill until the pepper looks a bit charred on bottom and the cheese is melted, about 20 minutes. Transfer to a serving platter with tongs, and enjoy.

# Chop Chop Salad Dressing Marinade
Serves 2 - 4

Sometimes recipes are the result of total accidents, like this one. I'd bought some cilantro for a recipe but hadn't used it all. Since I like cilantro--it's the spicey green that helps fire up Mexican food--I didn't want to waste it. So I chopped the leftovers and poured them into a jar with vinegar. (Vinegar is a preservative. I thought it would give me extra time to think about how to use it.) Well, I started using it as a salad dressing, mixing a bit of the cilantro-infused vinegar with a dab of mayonnaise. But I liked that so much, I wondered how it would be as a marinade. It was delicious.

## Ingredients
1/2 cup rice wine vinegar
1/4 cup oil
1/4 cup minced fresh cilantro
2 tablespoons chopped onion
4 cloves garlic, minced
1 pound venison steaks

## Preparation
1. Combine the vinegar, oil, cilantro, onion, and garlic 24 to 72 hours ahead of time. (You can even leave it longer; the vinegar will preserve the freshness.)
2. Place the venison steaks in a resealable plastic bag and pour the vinegar/cilantro marinade over them. Let them marinate in the refrigerator 24 to 48 hours.

## Cooking
1. Preheat the grill to medium-high heat. Let the steaks come to room temperature. Remove from the marinade, but don't dry or rinse the marinade off. That way, they won't stick to the cooking surface. Place on the grill and close the lid.
2. Cook until blood appears on the top of the steaks, then turn, and cook about half again as long. A 3/4-inch thick steak will take about 7-10 minutes, total for both sides, for medium rare.
3. Transfer to a heated platter. Serve hot.

****For even more heat, puree a 1 to 2-inch chunk of red onion, in the oil and vinegar before adding the cilantro and garlic.

# Zesty Dijon Salad Dressing Marinade

Here's another dressing that doubles--quite well--as a marinade, and this one was an accident, too. It started with Phil Shoemaker's homemade beer and a handful of opening day ptarmigan that needed cooking. The mustard just happened to be on the counter. It became a simple two-ingredient marinade, that suited the birds and the salad.

But, back home, I had no Phil beer. So I had to improvise, and with more time on my hands, it became a little more complex--but not much. I love the combination as both a dressing and a marinade for birds and big game. But I miss Phil's beer.

For dressing or marinade, combine the ingredients below in a small bowl and stir. Pour over your salad, or marinate a pound of elk, deer, antelope, or moose steaks--any venison will do--then go back to the Chop Chop cooking instructions for the rest.

1/4 cup mayonnaise
2 tablespoons prepared Dijon mustard
2 tablespoon rice wine vinegar
1/2 teaspoon sugar
1/4 teaspoon salt
1/4 teaspoon pepper

# Grilled Steaks with Chipotle Cream Sauce
Serves 2 - 4

This recipe is made specifically for all-outdoor cooking in the summertime, if you own a grill with a side burner. (I just got one two summers ago, so I'm way behind the curve on that.) If you don't have a side burner, make the sauce on the stove ahead of time--in a cast iron skillet--cover it with foil, and keep it warm on the edge of the grill until the steaks are done. To make timing easier, make up the Tex-Mex Potato Salad ahead of time and have it chilled and ready to go in your fridge.

## Ingredients
1 pound venison steaks
4 tablespoons butter
1/2 cup cream
2 tablespoons chipotle Tabasco sauce
1 ripe tomato, diced

## Cooking
1. Preheat the grill to medium-high heat. As the grill heats up, start the sauce.
2. Warm a skillet on your grill's side burner to medium-high heat. Add the butter, and when it has melted, add the cream and Chipotle sauce. Bring it to a very slow simmer, stirring often, and simmer about 2 minutes.
3. About the time you add the cream and Chipotle sauce to the butter, place the steaks on the grill and close the lid.
4. Cook them until blood appears on the top of the steaks, then turn, and cook about half again as long. A 3/4-inch thick steak will take about 7-10 minutes, total for both sides, for medium rare.
5. Transfer the steaks to the sauce pan on the side burner, spoon the sauce over them, strew the diced tomato over the sauce, and serve immediately.

# Gideon's Grub Rub Steaks
Serves 2-4

I named this spice rub mixture after our bird dog, Gideon, because it's also always ready to go. We use Gid's Rub on everything from pheasant to venison to fish. I've also sprinkled it on my Oven Fried Potatoes instead of the spices called for in that recipe. Just combine all the ingredients in a glass jar (or re-use an empty spice jar), cover tightly, and keep handy.

## Ingredients
2 tablespoons oil
1 tablespoon Gideon's Grub Rub
1 pound venison steaks

## Preparation
1. Mix the oil and Grub Rub (recipe below) in a resealable plastic bag.
2. Trim and dry the steaks and add to the marinade. Let marinate in the refrigerator for 4 to 24 hours.

## Cooking
1. Preheat the grill to medium-high heat. Let the steaks come to room temperature. Remove from the marinade, but don't dry or rinse the marinade off. That way, they won't stick to the cooking surface. Place on the grill and close the lid.
2. Cook until blood appears on the top of the steaks, then turn, and cook about half again as long. A 3/4-inch thick steak will take about 7-10 minutes, total for both sides, for medium rare.
3. Transfer to a heated platter. Serve hot, with Grilled Corn on the Cob.

## Gideon's Grub Rub
1/2 cup salt
1 1/2 teaspoons MSG
1 tablespoon coarse ground black pepper
2 tablespoons white sugar
1 tablespoon sweet paprika
3 tablespoons dried onion flakes
1 teaspoon garlic power

# Wild Sides: Grilled Corn on the Cob
Serves 4

Corn on the cob takes longer to cook than steaks and burgers. So give it a 10 minute head start before adding the meat to the grill.

## Ingredients
4 ears of fresh corn on the cob, with husks
2 tablespoons butter
2 tablespoons Gideon's Grub Rub

## Cooking
1. Preheat the grill to medium-high heat. Remove as much of the silk from the ears as you can, while leaving the husks attached. Rub the butter and sprinkle the Grub Rub over the ears, then close the husks as tight as possible over the corn. Tie a piece of string around the corn, if you'd like.
2. Place on the grill. Use long-handled tongs to turn them 3 times, to cook all sides evenly. The corn is done when it has browned kernels scattered around the ear. The husks, of course, will be toast. Remove the husks and serve the corn hot.

# Balsamic Parmesan Marinated Steaks
Serves 2-4

Grill these steaks outdoors, or pan-roast them indoors, then pair them with a season-appropriate potato dish—Josh's Sweet Potato Salad for summer, or Shiitake-Laced Scalloped Potatoes in winter.

## Ingredients
1/2 cup balsamic vinegar
1/4 cup oil
2-3 sprigs fresh thyme
1 sprig fresh oregano
1/4 cup grated Parmesan cheese
1/4 teaspoon salt
1/2 teaspoon coarse black pepper
1 pound venison steaks

## Preparation
1. Combine the vinegar, oil, thyme sprigs, oregano sprigs (stems and leaves intact), Parmesan, salt, and pepper in a resealable plastic bag.
2. Trim and dry the steaks, then add to the marinade. Let marinate 24 to 48 hours in the refrigerator.

## Grilling
1. Preheat the grill to medium-high heat. Remove the steaks from the marinade, but don't dry or rinse them off. That way, the meat won't stick to the cooking surface. Place on the grill and close the lid.
2. Cook until blood appears across the upper surface of the steaks, then turn, and cook about half again as long. A 3/4-inch thick steak will take about 7-10 minutes, total for both sides, for medium rare.

## Pan-Roasting:
1. Place cast iron skillet #1 in the center of your oven; preheat to 475°F. On the stovetop, bring one tablespoon of oil to a sizzle over medium-high heat in cast iron skillet #2 and sear the steaks on both sides, about 3 minutes. Transfer the steaks to skillet #1 to finish cooking: in ten minutes, a 3/4-inch steak should be a pink medium; a 1-inch steak, medium rare.
2. For a sauce: Lift skillet #2 off the stovetop burner a few seconds when you're done searing, lower the heat to medium-low, and pour the marinade into the pan. Simmer until the sauce thickens. Spoon the sauce over the steaks, and serve immediately.

## Tips & Tactics: What the Marinade Helps

Marinades can add both flavor and tenderness. The longer you marinate, the more effect, but it helps to start with a fairly good cut.

Meat that's been cold or muscle shortened won't benefit by aging, cooking, or marinating as much as meat that starts out moderately tender.

Male mule deer, elk, and caribou taken in the rut are often better left to the sausage maker than the more delicate flavorings of a marinade.

So evaluate just how much you're expecting that marinade to accomplish. If you're looking for tweaking, fine. If you're looking for an entire remodel, make sausage instead. Even a rutty old buck can make succulent brats and sausage.

# Pomegranate Balsamic Vinegar Marinated Steaks
Serves 4

My local kitchen store carries a handful of Cuisine Perel brand vinegars, and as I've experimented with them I've grown to love how easy it is to make complexly flavored marinades with very few ingredients. It's as easy as opening a bottle, yet a lot more satisfying than an Italian dressing marinade. (Not that there's anything wrong with Italian dressing. Just not every time.) If you can't find Cuisine Perel go to www.cuisineperel.com; they sell directly from the web site.

## Ingredients
1/2 cup pomegranate balsamic vinegar
1/4 cup oil
1/2 teaspoon salt
1/2 teaspoon coarse black pepper
1 pound venison steaks or 2-inch chunks for kabobs

## Preparation
1. Combine the vinegar, oil, salt, and pepper in a resealable plastic bag. Trim the steaks, dry with paper towels, and add to the marinade.
2. Let marinate in the refrigerator for 24 to 48 hours. (The tougher the steaks, or the more tenderizing you want, the longer the marinade.)

## Cooking
1. Preheat the grill to medium-high heat. Let the steaks come to room temperature. Remove from the marinade, but don't dry or rinse the marinade off. That way, the meat won't stick to the grill. Place on the grill and close the lid.
2. Cook until blood appears on the top of the steaks, then turn, and cook about half again as long. A 3/4-inch thick steak will take about 7-10 minutes, total for both sides, for medium rare.
3. Transfer to a heated platter. Serve hot, with the Grilled Cherry Tomatoes.

## Wild Sides: Grilled Cherry Tomatoes

The best way I've found to get the sweet grill flavor without sacrificing tomatoes to the fire is to cook them in an aluminum foil 'boat' on one corner of the grill. A double layer of foil will do, with the edges folded up an inch or so to keep the juices--and tomatoes--from rolling off.

Put the tomatoes on the grill when you start the steaks, and roll them around in their life boat with a spatula 2 to 3 times until slightly browned. Steaks, kabobs, pheasant breasts, they all take about the same time as the tomatoes, no matter what temperature you choose, so everything's hot and at the table together.

To remove the boat from the grill, use long-armed hot mitts, fold the boat up and in toward the center and slide it onto a platter. Salt, pepper or even a bit of barbecue sauce are optional. Cherry tomatoes are magnificent grilled, without any help at all.

# Bacon-Wrapped Medallions
Serves 4-5

The most tender steak of all isn't even a steak. Medallions are just the tenderloin cut across the grain into steak-thick pieces you can then cook like steaks. For a well-rounded medallion, choose a deer tenderloin of a mature deer; if you're lucky enough to have a bit of moose or elk in the freezer, the hanging tenderloins are large enough for medallions, too.

## Ingredients
10-inch strip of tenderloin, trimmed
4-5 slices bacon
Salt and pepper to taste

## Cooking
1. Preheat the grill to medium heat. Slice the tenderloin into 1 to 1 1/2-inch thick medallions--about the thickness of the slice of bacon you're about to wrap around it. Wrap and secure the bacon with a toothpick. Rub a little oil on the top and bottom of the medallion.
2. Place the meat on the grill and cook about 15 minutes, flip and cook about 7 more minutes. If the bacon isn't done, tip the medallion on its side and roll across the fire to brown the bacon.
3. Sprinkle with a bit of salt and pepper and serve immediately with a potato salad or this Savory Pasta.

## Tips & Tactics: Grilling Temperature
If you can comfortably hold your hand just over the cooking surface for 2 to 3 seconds, the fire's hot; 4-5 seconds, it's medium; 6-7 seconds, it's low. On an oven thermometer, with the lid closed, high is about 500°F; medium about 350°F; low about 250°F.

And, please, this isn't an endurance test. Remove your hand when it gets too warm.

## Wild Sides: Savory Pasta
Serves 2-3

Bob's Thriftway doesn't carry orzo pasta or radicchio, but he only caters to the 2,000 people in my home town. If I drive 35 miles, to a town of 25,000, radicchio sits between the romaine lettuce and vine-ripened tomatoes. The orzo is one aisle over with the spaghetti.

## Ingredients
2 tablespoons butter
1 ounce ham, minced
1/2 cup red onion, sliced
1/2 sweet red bell pepper, diced
3 cloves garlic, minced
1 tablespoon chopped sun-dried tomatoes
2 cups cooked orzo pasta
1/2 cup sliced raw spinach
1/2 cup sliced radicchio

## Cooking
1. In a skillet, melt the butter over medium heat and sauté the ham, red onion, red pepper, and garlic together.
2. When the ham begins to brown and the onion to soften, stir in the sun-dried tomatoes, and cooked orzo. Toss until all the ingredients are sizzling hot, then add the spinach and radicchio, letting them get warm but not much else. Serve immediately.

Slice Of The Wild

# Hot & Sweet Venison Kabobs
Serves 2-4

This is a simple marinade paired with grilled vegetables, a favorite summer dinner of mine. The thing is that it's not only tasty, but bringing a bevy of kabobs to the table laden with grilled meat and vegetables will impress the most jaded of appetites. This way, it's also simple to do. You can also use tender chunks for any kabob or stir-fry recipe, if you've got some left in the freezer. And as for the elephant garlic? Imagine a head of regular garlic is a squirrel--then blow it up to the size of an elephant. It's much milder in flavor, and much easier to stick on a skewer.

## Ingredients
1 pound venison steaks, cut in 2" chunks
1 red onion, quartered
1/2 cup rice wine vinegar
1/2 cup oil
1/4 cup Louisiana hot sauce
1/4 cup honey
1/4 teaspoon salt
1/4 teaspoon coarse black pepper
1 head of elephant garlic, separated and peeled

## Preparation
1. Trim the steak chunks, and dry with paper towels.
2. Puree 1/4 of the onion in a food processor with the oil, vinegar, hot sauce, honey, salt, and pepper. Pour into a resealable plastic bag. Add the steaks. Marinate 24 to 48 hours in the refrigerator.

## Cooking
1. Preheat your grill to medium-high heat. Cut the rest of the onion into bite-sized chunks, and the elephant garlic into thick slices.
2. Remove the meat chunks from the marinade without rinsing or drying them, and place on skewers, alternating chunks of red onion and slices of garlic with the meat.
2. Place the kabobs on the grill, and cook for 3-4 minutes on the first side. Turn, and cook about the same on the second side. Cut a piece of meat off the skewer to test for doneness.

## Wild Sides: Doctor E-Z Beans
Ever since the makers of Tabasco Sauce came out with the new smoked variety--Chipotle--we've been finding all kinds of ways to use it. This is just one of many.

15 ounce can Van Camp's pork and beans
1/2 teaspoon chili powder
2 teaspoons molasses
2 teaspoons maple syrup
1 teaspoon Chipotle Tabasco sauce

Combine all the ingredients, heat on high in a microwave --or over a campfire--until bubbly hot.

## Tips and Tactics: Is Wood Better?
When using metal skewers, it's safest to remove the meat and grilled vegetables from the skewers before serving simply because metal doesn't cool down very quickly.

Wooden skewers cool quickly but need to be soaked 30 minutes before grilling so they don't burn up on the grill. They also have a tendency to splinter. (A safety factor at the table.)

Wooden skewers are cheap, but metal is reusable, almost infinitely. If you kabob a few times a year, choose wood. If you kabob a lot or have small kids, metal is a better choice.

# Chili-on-a-Stick
Serves 6-8

This is one of my favorite dinners, perfect for a hot summer night or last-blast barbecue before winter forces us indoors. Pair it with this Tex-Mex Potato Salad or with Two-Can Baked Beans. Since kabob chunks tend to vary in size, it's best to group larger chunks on one skewer, smaller ones on another. Then test for doneness by slicing into the end piece.

## Ingredients
- 2 pounds venison steaks, in 2-inch chunks
- 1/4 cup red wine vinegar
- 1/2 cup apple juice
- 1/2 cup oil
- 1/4 cup minced onion
- 2 cloves garlic, minced
- 1/2 teaspoon chili powder
- 1 tablespoon minced fresh cilantro
- 1/2 teaspoon salt
- 1 teaspoon black pepper
- 6 whole fresh jalapeno peppers
- 12 large-bulbed green onions
- 1 pound cherry tomatoes
- 1/2 cup mesquite wood chips (optional)

## Preparation
1. Trim and dry the steaks. In a resealable plastic bag mix the vinegar, apple juice, oil, onion, garlic, chili powder, cilantro, salt, and pepper. Add the steaks and let them marinate in the refrigerator 2 to 4 hours.
2. Soak the mesquite chips in water 30 minutes. Prepare the vegetables for the skewers: split and seed the jalapenos, then cut them in half lengthwise. Trim the onions. Drain the meat from the marinade and arrange on the skewers, alternating meat with the vegetables.

## Cooking
1. Preheat the grill to medium-hot; place the mesquite on the coals.
2. When the fire is ready, place the kabobs on the grill. Cover and cook about 4 minutes, turn, then continue cooking another 4 minutes. Serve with lots of Tex-Mex Potato Salad, corn chips, fresh salsa, and ice cold beer.

## Wild Sides: Tex-Mex Potato Salad
Serves 6

If you have a bottle of pickled peppers, just pour off a bit of the vinegar: that's what I'm calling chili vinegar. Or, start your own bottle just for the vinegar. Fill a pint jar with an assortment of chiles: serranos and habaneros for heat, one Anaheim for mellow flavor. Then fill with rice wine vinegar, cover and chill.

### Ingredients
- 1 1/2 pound potatoes
- 2 eggs
- 1/2 yellow onion, chopped
- 1/2 cup mayonnaise
- 1 1/2 tablespoons chili vinegar
- 1/4 cup minced fresh cilantro
- 1 teaspoon chili powder
- 1/2 teaspoon ground cumin

### Preparation
1. Boil the potatoes until just fork-tender. (About 20 minutes for medium sized potatoes; more for bigger ones.) Hard-boil the eggs. Cool both with cold running water, then chill 1 to 2 hours.
2. Chop the chilled potatoes and eggs into a large bowl with the onion. In a small bowl combine the mayonnaise, chili vinegar, cilantro, chili powder, and cumin. Gently toss the mayonnaise mixture into the potatoes. Cover, chill, and then serve.

# Old World Marinated Venison and Potato Kabobs
Serves 2-4

For those who don't cotton to super-sweet barbecue sauces, this mustard sauce makes a vibrant statement. And the real joy of this recipe is it's a grilled version of a one-dish meal. No sides required.

## Ingredients
1 pound venison, cut into 2-inch chunks
1/4 cup malt vinegar
2 tablespoons brown sugar
2 tablespoons prepared Dijon mustard
2 tablespoons oil
1/2 teaspoon coarse black pepper
1 pound new red potatoes
1 red onion, sliced thick
4 slices bacon

## Preparation
1. Trim the steak chunks, and dry with paper towels.
2. In a resealable plastic bag combine the vinegar, sugar, mustard, oil, and pepper. Add the meat, and refrigerate 24 to 48 hours.

## Cooking
1. Preheat the grill to medium-high heat.
2. Microwave the potatoes on high for about 2 minutes, or until just fork tender, but still firm enough to be able to put on the skewer. Remove the meat from the marinade and arrange on the skewers, alternating with the potatoes and onion slices and threading the bacon along the skewer as you add ingredients.
3. Cook about 2 minutes a side, until the bacon is browned all over, turning four times. Remove from the skewers and serve hot, with more mustard.

****New potatoes are the golf-ball sized, first-picked potatoes that show up in the produce section in early summer. You can cut up mature potatoes for these kabobs, but new potatoes have better flavor and don't need any prep.

## Red Wine Marinated Venison Kabobs
Serves 4

The thing about kabobs is that with the meat in smaller chunks, the marinade really gets a chance to permeate every fiber. Plus, kabobs cook faster than steaks or roasts. And who doesn't enjoy popping a piece of delicately cooked meat in their mouth--fresh off the grill? Just leave enough for everyone else. Of course any of these kabob marinades can be used for steaks and vice versa.

### Ingredients
1/2 cup dry red wine (Merlot or Cabernet works)
2 tablespoons oil
2 tablespoons minced shallots
1/2 teaspoon minced garlic
1 teaspoon salt
1/2 teaspoon white pepper
1 pound venison steak, cut in 2-inch chunks

### Preparation
1. Combine the wine, oil, shallots, garlic, salt, and pepper in a resealable plastic bag.
2. Trim the steak chunks, and dry with paper towels. Add to the marinade, and marinate in the refrigerator for 24 to 48 hours. (The tougher the meat, or the more tenderizing you want, the longer the marinade.)

### Cooking
1. Preheat the grill to medium-high heat. Remove the meat chunks from the marinade without rinsing or drying them, and place on skewers, leaving a little space between the chunks of meat. (Save the marinade. It can be re-used for up to 5 days.)
2. Place the kabobs on the grill, and cook for 3-4 minutes on the first side. Turn, and cook about the same on the second side. Remove from the heat and serve.

## Wild Sides: Four Bean Salad
Serves 8

Hot weather demands flavors that cut though the doldrums. Four-bean salad is a classic cure.

### Ingredients
15 ounce can black beans
15 ounce can pinto beans
15 ounce can kidney beans
15 ounce can yellow wax beans
1 red sweet bell pepper, quartered
1/2 medium red onion, quartered
1/2 cup oil
1/2 cup apple cider vinegar
1/2 cup sugar
1 tablespoon dry mustard
1 teaspoon salt
1/2 teaspoon pepper

### Preparation
1. Drain, rinse and combine the beans. Put the rest of the ingredients in a food processor and pulse 2-3 seconds until the onion and peppers are coarsely chopped.
2. Pour the chopped onion/peppers mixture over the beans, toss, cover and refrigerate. Serve chilled.

Slice Of The Wild

# Blood Orange Marinated Kabobs
Serves 2-4

Like the pomegranate balsamic vinegar, I found the blood orange vinegar in my local kitchen store. I started using it in Hungarian partridge and pheasant marinades, then found I liked it just as well on venison. Flavored vinegars are one of the easiest ways I know to make 2 to 4 ingredient marinate taste complicated and exotic. You don't even have to tell anyone where you got it. If you can't find any in your stores, buy it at www.cuisineperel.com.

## Ingredients
1/2 cup blood orange vinegar
1/4 cup oil
6 bay leaves
1/2 teaspoon salt
1/2 teaspoon coarse black pepper
1 pound venison steaks, in 2-inch chunks

## Preparation
1. Process the vinegar, oil, bay leaves, salt, and pepper in a blender until the bay leaves are very small bits. Transfer to a resealable plastic bag.
2. Trim the steaks, and dry with paper towels. Add to the marinade, and let marinate in the refrigerator for 24 to 48 hours. (The tougher the steaks or the more flavor you want, the longer the marinade.)

## Cooking
1. Preheat the grill to medium-high heat. Remove the meat chunks from the marinade, pluck any bay leaf chips from the meat, but don't rinse or dry it. Place on skewers, leaving space between the chunks of meat. (Save the marinade. It can be re-used for up to 5 days.)
2. Place the kabobs on the grill, and cook for 3-4 minutes on the first side. Turn, and cook about the same on the second side. Slice into an end piece to check for doneness. These do cook very fast, and no dry-cooked game should be taken past medium if you want it to be tender and moist.

## Tips & Tactics: When Is It Done?
The easiest way to test steaks and kabobs for doneness is to slice a bit off an end and simply look at it. Large roasts still need a meat thermometer stuck in the middle, but for the rest, you can tell enough from one slice to know if you need to stop cooking right now, or let it cook longer.

In cross-section:
Bloody rare: the meat is almost purple and all but the seared edges look raw.
Rare: red in the center, running to pink around that, with the seared outside.
Medium rare: reddish-pink fairly evenly, but juices flow easily when you cut into it.
Medium: some red in the very center, but it's a darker, dryer red, and much less juice runs when you cut into it.

For best results with game, no dry-cooked meat should be taken much past medium if you want it to be tender and moist. Leaving at least a little pink ensures more tender results. (Dry-cooking is anything cooked without liquids including grilling, pan-roasting, roasting in the oven without gravy or sauce. Save well done for pot roasts, cover & bake, and braising dishes.)

# Kabobs with Tangy Peanut Marinade and Dipping Sauce
Serves 2-4

John keeps Mae Ploy's sweet chili sauce on hand at all times. It's hot, like tabasco, but mellow, if that's possible, and available in the Asian/ethnic section in bigger grocery stores. I've used this peanut sauce on both venison and birds and it works well for both. The sweet chili sauce also works as a bird marinade by itself--or with an equal amount of orange juice. For safety's sake with any marinade, don't add the marinade you had the meat in to the cold dip you serve at the table. If it had any stomach-churning bugs, they will transfer, alive and well, to the dip, and you will rue the day. To re-use any marinade as a cold dipping sauce, boil it for 4 minutes first. A gentle simmer is hot enough, but make sure it goes the full 4 minutes. Then pour it into a Pyrex container, cover, and set in the freezer to chill out while everything else cooks. It doesn't take long to chill out in the freezer.

## Ingredients
5 tablespoons sweet chili sauce
3 tablespoons soy sauce
2 tablespoons creamy peanut butter
3 tablespoons coconut milk
10-12 wooden skewers
1 pound steaks, cut in 1/2" thick strips

## Preparation
1. Combine the sweet chili sauce, soy sauce, peanut butter, and coconut milk in a blender, and puree 4-5 seconds until smooth.
2. Divide the mixture equally: pour one half into a resealable plastic bag large enough to hold the meat, and then add the meat and marinate overnight. Pour the second half into a jar for a dipping sauce. Refrigerate both.

## Cooking
1. Soak the wooden skewers in cold water for 30 minutes. Preheat the grill to medium-high.
2. Remove the meat from the marinade without rinsing or drying it. Thread each steak strip onto a skewer loosely, and cook about 5-8 minutes, turning once.
3. Serve hot with the well-chilled--and safe to eat--dipping sauce. Left on the skewer, it's almost like chewing on a drumstick.

****Oddly enough our little grocery store in Townsend stocks the more common Thai hot chili sauce; so when I can't get Mae Ploy's sweet version, I substitute 2 tablespoons of the hot chili sauce mixed with 2 tablespoons water and 4 tablespoons sugar. It's pretty close.

## Wild Sides: What Goes With?
This peanut sauce is a vibrant marinade and dip, so you can go two ways. Either match it with another vibrant sauce containing similar spices, or go with a contrasting cooler flavor.

Curried Potato Salad or Sweet and Sour Slaw would be a complement; while the Traditional Potato Salad and Scalloped Pineapple would be a tasty contrast. It's up to you. Personally, I think Scalloped Pineapple goes with everything. Check the table of contents for page numbers.

# Tasty Quesadillas
Serves 4

As simple as a grilled cheese sandwich, yet so much more in flavor. A quesadilla makes a great lunch anytime, anywhere. To make it easier, use bottled or store-bought salsa, but for a flavor bump, take a few minutes to make your own. If you garden, and have a bumper crop of tomatoes, salsa is a no-cook cure that goes down really easily.

## Ingredients
1 pound tender venison steaks
3 tablespoons oil, in all
8 corn tortillas
1 cup sour cream
1 cup fresh or bottled salsa
1 cup grated Cheddar cheese

## Cooking
1. Preheat the oven to 250°F. Place a cookie sheet in the center of the oven.
2. In a large skillet over medium-high heat, cook the steaks in one tablespoon of the oil, turning them when the blood appears across the top of the steak, and cooking until rare to medium rare. Transfer to a plate to cool. (Don't cover them.)
3. Arrange 4 of the tortillas on a cutting board. Slice the venison steak thin, across the grain, and mix with the sour cream, salsa, and Cheddar cheese in a large bowl. Divide into four parts and spread onto the first four tortillas. Cover with the other four tortillas.
4. Heat the skillet again with another tablespoon of oil over medium-high heat. Cook the layered tortillas in the skillet one at a time, as for a grilled cheese sandwich, turning once after the bottoms are lightly browned. Transfer each to the cookie sheet in the oven while you finish cooking the rest. Cut in quarters, like a pizza, and serve hot with lots of corn chips.
****If you prefer, grill the steaks outdoors instead of frying them indoors. Just substitute the grilling instructions from another steak recipe. And to add more heat, substitute Pepper Jack cheese for the cheddar.

## Wild Sides: Fresh Salsa
If John's cooking, there's more jalapeno, and everything is chopped by hand; I'm prone to 'pulsing' everything in the food processor, and switching out the jalapeno for milder Anaheims or more complex serrano peppers. (I'm also more careful about removing the seeds and spines--with rubber gloves on. That's where a lot of the heat is.)

We both will throw in a clove of garlic or two and a little lime juice when we're not in a big hurry. Now and then I 'chipotle' the pepper by holding it over a gas burner, with tongs, until the skin is blistered and small black spots show up here and there. Toss the pepper into a plastic bag until it cools, then peel, chop, and add it to the salsa. Here's the basic quick-time recipe we've used for years.

## Ingredients
3 cups diced vine-ripened tomato
1 cup diced yellow onion
1 jalapeno pepper, diced
2 tablespoons minced fresh cilantro

## Preparation
Combine all the ingredients in a glass jar, cover, chill, and serve. Makes about 1 pint.

# Ten Minute Steaks with Herbed Madeira Sauce

Serves 4

This is one of several recipes I've used for cooking demonstrations--one time, famously, for a morning TV host in Chicago. She was one of those ultra-urban young people who thought game meat was alien bio-matter, and had her face all screwed up before she even picked up the fork. Then she tasted it, and said, "That's wild?" Hunters respond in a similar way, except their question is always: "You didn't marinate that?" But not like it? Never. (Do, however read about cooking with spirits first.)

## Ingredients
1 pound tender venison steaks
2 tablespoons oil
1/4 cup Madeira
2 tablespoons butter
1 tablespoon chopped fresh basil
1 tablespoon chopped fresh oregano
1 green onion, chopped
1/4 teaspoon pepper
1/4 teaspoon salt

## Cooking
1. Place a platter in the oven and preheat to 200°F. Prepare the steaks by trimming, then drying them with paper towels.
2. In a large skillet, heat the oil over medium high heat, then add the steaks. Cook on the first side until you see blood on the top surface. Turn, and cook about half again as long. Pull the heated platter from the oven, transfer the steaks to it, and cover with foil.
3. Remove the pan from the burner just long enough to pour the Madeira into a measuring cup. (Don't pour it directly into the hot pan.)
4. Return the pan to the heat, and deglaze the pan with the Madeira, letting it bubble down to about half the volume.
5. Add the rest of the ingredients, stirring to mix the herbs into the butter, and simmer 1-2 minutes. Pour the sauce over the steaks and serve with Super Creamy Mac & Cheese, Traditional Potato Salad, or Savory Rice.

## Tips & Tactics: Cooking with Spirits

This is a perfectly safe recipe for even a novice cook as long as you pre-measure. Spirits have alcohol, something we forget when we're cooking with them since a few seconds after they hit the hot pan, the alcohol disappears.

Well, where did it go? That's a pertinent question. Adding alcohol to a very hot pan, as you could do in this recipe--is likely to show you exactly where the alcohol goes: up in a ball of flames.

I've even had wine go up in a ball of flames, but the higher the alcohol content of the liquid, and the higher the temperature of the pan, the higher the potential for disaster. The extreme? The flames can ride back up the stream back into the bottle and--BOOM--the bottle explodes in your hand.

So, take two safety steps:
1. Remove the pan from the heat before adding alcohol. Five to ten seconds is all it takes to safely add spirits.
2. Pour the spirits into a measuring cup before adding them to the pan. Wine has less alcohol content than Madeira (a fortified wine), which has less than hard liquor, like whiskey. But all are potential flame-throwers, given enough heat.

# Quick Italian Tender Chunks
Serves 4

You remember tender chunks from the hind quarter butchering pages? They're the bite-sized chunks of meat that get left behind when you cut your tenderloins, rump steaks, and roasts off the bone. They're just as good to eat as those steaks and roasts, but often get thrown into the burger pile. At our house we label them 'tender chunks' and use them for quick-cooking, small-bite dishes: kabobs, stir-fries, and this quick Italian job. For tougher chunks, add 1 cup beef bouillon with the tomatoes and let the dish simmer about 45 minutes longer.

## Ingredients
1 pound bite-sized tender chunks
1 cup Contadina Italian flavored bread crumbs
2 tablespoons oil
14.5 ounce can Italian recipe diced tomatoes
4 cloves garlic, minced
1/4 teaspoon salt
1/4 teaspoon coarse black pepper
1/2 cup grated Parmesan cheese

## Cooking
1. Roll the tender chunks in the bread crumbs. In a 3-quart Dutch oven, heat the oil over medium heat, and sauté the breaded chunks until lightly browned.
2. Add the tomatoes with all their liquid, plus the garlic, salt, and pepper to the browned meat. Cover, and reduce the heat to low. Simmer about 20 minutes, covered, until tender. Serve with plain pasta or this Sautéed Pepper and Onions and more Parmesan cheese.

****For a tasty variation, caramelize one yellow onion in a separate skillet as the meat cooks. Spoon on top of the meat when serving. To caramelize: sauté the onion over medium-low heat in 2 tablespoons of oil until it is very sweet and lightly browned, about 20 minutes. (You can help it along by adding 1 teaspoon of sugar at the start.)

# Wild Sides: Sautéed Pepper and Onions

Sauté is just a fancy word for fry, lightly, which is what turns these most common of veggies into a side dish that stand up to these Italian Tender Chunks or ends up piled high on a tasty venison burger. The fire roasted red peppers in this recipe are a fairly new item in the Safeway store brands: they come three to a 12 ounce jar, and really add a punch to very simple dishes.

## Ingredients
2 tablespoons oil
1 yellow onion, sliced
1 red bell pepper, sliced
1 to 2 fire roasted red bell peppers
1 stalk broccoli, cut into florets

## Cooking
1. In a large skillet (10-inch) heat the oil over medium heat until just smoking, then add all the vegetables. Gently stir them as they sauté and reduce in volume by about 1/3.
2. Sauté until the onions are soft, very bright in color, and starting to look 'together,' about 15 minutes. Serve hot as a side dish, or as a hot veggie relish for burgers on a bun.

# Asian-American Stir-Fry
Serves 4

This is a tasty, quick, sweet and sour stir-fry that seems familiar but has an edge that makes it special. Use a wok if you have it, or a heavy-bottomed skillet. Cast iron works well. And feel free to use this marinade on plain old grilled steaks. It's that wonderful combination of sweet and tangy.

## Ingredients
1/4 cup oyster sauce
1/4 cup soy sauce
1/4 cup honey
1/2 cup rice wine vinegar
4 teaspoons grated ginger
1 pound moderately tender venison
2 tablespoons oil
1 yellow onion, chopped
1 red sweet Bell pepper, chopped
8 ounces snow pea pods

## Preparation
1. Combine the oyster sauce, soy sauce, honey, vinegar and grated ginger in a resealable plastic bag.
2. Slice the venison into thin strips and add to the marinade bag. Refrigerate overnight.

## Cooking
1. Heat the oil over medium-high heat in a large wok or cast iron skillet. When it's hot, stir-fry the marinated venison until lightly browned, 2-3 minutes. Add the vegetables and stir them into the meat, letting them cook until the onions are lightly browned. Add the marinade and stir it into the meat and vegetables.
3. Let the dish continue to cook until the volume of the sauce is reduced by about half. Serve over rice.

# Very-Asian Stir-Fry
Serves 4

For those who are looking for a more adventurous sauce, this Asian stir-fry is perfect. The toasted sesame seed oil is very earthy and the Thai sweet chili sauce is bright and sharp--a perfect combination of yin and yang. Five years ago, this may have been pretty exotic. But these days, I find all these ingredients are available in the 'ethnic' section of the grocery store in Helena, Montana--my 'big' grocery store. Add more chili sauce at the table if you want; it really is the spark in the sauce.

## Ingredients
1/4 cup toasted sesame seed oil, in all
1/4 cup Thai sweet chili sauce, in all
2 teaspoons black bean garlic sauce
1 pound steaks or tender chunks
1/2 cup beef stock
1 teaspoon corn starch
2 stalks celery, chopped
1 small yellow onion, chopped
1 sweet red bell pepper, chopped
4 green onions, diced

## Preparation
1. Combine the oil, 2 tablespoons of the Thai chili sauce, and the black bean sauce in a resealable plastic bag.
2. Slice the steak pieces into thin strips and add to the marinade bag. Refrigerate overnight.

## Cooking
1. Combine the other 2 tablespoons of Thai sweet chili sauce with the beef stock and corn starch. Stir to dissolve the corn starch and set aside. This is the finishing sauce.
2. Start a cast iron skillet over medium high heat, and when the skillet's hot, add the marinated meat. Don't pour the excess marinade into the pan; but, also, don't wipe the oil off the meat. It subs for more oil in the pan for sautéing.
3. Brown the first side of the meat, about 2-3 minutes, then turn, and add the celery, onion, and pepper. Stir to blend the flavors and continue cooking until the onions start to brown.
4. Add the finishing sauce to the pan and simmer until it has thickened up a bit, about 3 minutes. Serve over rice, with the diced green onions strewn across the top. For those who prefer lots of heat, serve more Thai sauce at the table, and add at will.

# Pan-Roasted Steaks in Citrus Marinade

Serves 3-4

Yes, you'll get two skillets dirty. And, while rare and medium rare steaks are lip-drooling good, pan roasting makes a juicy, flavorful steak, even when you go all the way to medium. In hot weather, serve with Grilled Corn on the Cob, Sweet And Sour Slaw, Red Ranch Rotini Salad, or Roundup Salad. In cold weather, Two-Can Baked Beans or Sweet Rice will keep you going. Check the table of contents for page numbers.

## Ingredients

1 1/2 cups orange juice
2 tablespoons lime juice
2 cloves minced garlic
2 tablespoons red wine vinegar
1 pound tender steaks or medallions
1 tablespoon oil

## Preparation

1. Combine the orange juice, lime juice, garlic, and vinegar in a resealable plastic bag.
2. Add the steaks to the marinade, and refrigerate overnight.

## Cooking

1. Place cast iron skillet #1 in the center of your oven; preheat to 475°F. On the stovetop, bring one tablespoon of oil to a sizzle over medium-high heat in cast iron skillet #2. Remove the steaks from the marinade and sear the steaks on both sides, about 3 minutes.
2. Transfer the steaks to skillet #1 to finish cooking: in ten minutes, a 3/4-inch steak should be medium (and still a little pink); a 1-inch steak, medium rare.
2. For a sauce: Lift skillet #2 off the stovetop burner a few seconds when you're done searing, lower the heat to medium-low, and pour the marinade into the pan. Simmer until the sauce thickens, or the steaks are done. Spoon the sauce over the steaks, and serve immediately.

## Tips & Tactics: Cooking Temperature

You'll notice sometimes the pan-roasting calls for a 475°F oven and sometimes a 250°F oven. The answer is in how long it takes to cook the sauce. The point is to have both sauce and steak done at the same time, but not waste time either. So how long should it take to cook sauce?

There are no timed events in sauce cooking. Perhaps your kitchen has more distractions than mine--like small children. If you find the 475° finishes the steaks too fast and is stressing you out, lower the oven to 250°F. Cooking should be fun, not stressful.

Slice Of The Wild

# Pan-Roasted Steaks with Mushroom Sauce
Serves 2-4

Pan-roasting is a combination of searing in a skillet, then finishing the cooking in the oven. It's the most predictable way I know to get moist venison steaks, even if you cook them until all the pink is gone. Plus, it's very quick. Be sure to have all your prep work done before starting the pans.

## Ingredients
1 pound steaks, about 3/4-inch thick
5 tablespoons butter
2 cloves garlic, minced
4 ounces mushrooms, sliced
1/4 cup Marsala wine
3 green onions, chopped

## Cooking
1. Trim and dry the steaks with paper towels.
2. Chop and measure the rest of the ingredients, so they're ready to go. (Always pour spirits into a measuring cup first, rather than pouring them direct from the bottle into a hot skillet.)
3. Place cast iron skillet #1 in the center of your oven; preheat to 475°F. On the stovetop, bring 2 tablespoons of the butter to a sizzle over medium-high heat in cast iron skillet #2 and sear the steaks on both sides, about 3 minutes.
4. Transfer the steaks to skillet #1 to finish cooking: in ten minutes, a 3/4- inch steak should be a slightly pink medium; a 1-inch steak, medium rare. Remove the searing pan from the heat for 30 seconds, then continue.
5. Add the rest of the butter to the pan, lower the heat to medium, and sauté the garlic and mushrooms for about 3 minutes or until tender. Add the wine and green onions to the mushrooms and return the steaks to the pan. Spoon the sauce over the steaks a few times, then transfer to a preheated platter and serve.

# Wild Sides: Super Creamy Mac & Cheese
4-6 servings

Use the best cheese the world has to offer, or the generic store brand variety—doesn't matter. It will still be galaxies better than boxed macaroni & cheese.

## Ingredients
3 tablespoons flour
1 cup milk
3 tablespoons butter or margarine
4 ounces cream cheese, room temperature, in chunks
1 mounded cup mozzarella cheese, coarsely grated
8 ounces rotini, cooked and drained
3 tablespoons Italian seasoned bread crumbs
3 tablespoons grated Parmesan cheese

## Cooking
1. Preheat the oven to 350°F.
2. In a microwave-safe medium-sized bowl, whip the flour into the milk until there are no lumps. Add the butter. Microwave on high about 1 ½ to 2 minutes, until the mixture comes to a boil. (Start with the time it takes your microwave to boil water; then watch so it doesn't boil over.)
3. Stir in the cream cheese: microwave another 15 seconds to reheat. Now stir in the mozzarella.
3. Gently fold the cheese sauce into the rotini, and then pour it all into a 9-inch square baking dish. Stir the bread crumbs and Parmesan cheese together and sprinkle over the top. Bake, uncovered, for 20 minutes. Serve hot.

# Pan-Roasted Steaks in Creamy Garlic Sauce
Serves 2-4

Made with milder flavored elephant garlic, this creamy sauce cooks up in the pan quickly, and has a zesty, but not overpowering, garlic flavor. Since this cooks up quickly, the steaks need to be tender: take them from the upper rump, or perhaps medallions cut from the tenderloin or hanging tenderloin

## Ingredients
1 pound tender venison steaks, 3/4-inch thick
1 tablespoon oil
2 tablespoons butter
3/4 cup dry red wine (Merlot or Cabernet will work)
1/2 cup minced elephant garlic (about 2 cloves)
3/4 cup cream
3/4 cup chopped Roma tomatoes
2 tablespoons chopped fresh sweet basil
1/4 teaspoon white pepper

## Cooking
1. Prepare the steaks by trimming them and drying with paper towels. Set aside. Get two cast iron skillets out.
2. Chop and measure all the rest of the ingredients, so they're ready to go. (Always pour spirits into a measuring cup, rather than pouring them direct from the bottle to a hot skillet.)
3. Place cast iron skillet #1 in the center of your oven; preheat to 475°F. On the stovetop, bring the oil and butter to a sizzle over medium-high heat in cast iron skillet #2 and sear the steaks on both sides, about 3 minutes. Transfer the steaks to skillet #1 to finish cooking; in ten minutes, a 3/4-inch steak should be a slightly pink medium; a 1-inch steak, medium rare.
4. Remove pan #2 from the heat for 5 to 10 seconds, then pour the wine into the pan, turning the heat down to medium low, or whatever will keep the wine at a gentle simmer. Stir in the garlic and cream. Continue to simmer until the wine sauce is reduced by about half; add the tomatoes, basil and pepper, and return the steaks to the sauce. Spoon the sauce over the steaks, 2-3 minutes, until well coated. Transfer the steaks to the plates, and pour the sauce over them. Serve immediately.

## Tips & Tactics: A Perfect Finish
For best results when pan-roasting, sear the steaks for about 3 minutes--for both sides--then continue cooking them in the oven for up to 10 minutes.

The longer you leave them in the oven the more done they will be, but at 475°F, 10 minutes will cook a 1-inch thick steak a still pinkish medium rare.

And how will you tell when they're done? The easiest way is to take a thin slice off one end and simply look at it. The steaks will still be moist--and you've eliminated the guess work.

# Pan-Roasted Safari Steaks
Serves 6-8

This is a recipe we've been using for so long I've forgotten why we started calling them safari steaks. Maybe we ate something like this on safari? Maybe it just makes us feel like we're not eating at home? I just know they taste great with Oven Fried Potatoes. They're also good with Half-Mashed Potatoes and Irish Mashed Potatoes.

## Ingredients
2 pounds venison steaks, 3/4-inch thick
2 tablespoons oil
2 tablespoons butter
1 to 2 tablespoons black pepper
1 cup dry red wine
1 cup ruby port
2 cloves garlic, minced
4 tablespoons tomato paste
1 tablespoon apple juice concentrate
1 tablespoon red currant jelly

## Cooking
1. Dry the steaks and trim any rough edges.
2. Place cast iron skillet #1 in the center of your oven; preheat to 475°F. On the stovetop, bring the oil and butter to a sizzle over medium-high heat in cast iron skillet #2 and sear the steaks on both sides, about 3 minutes. Transfer the steaks to skillet #1 and sprinkle with pepper.
3. Take skillet #2 off the heat for 10 seconds., then add the red wine, port, garlic, tomato paste, apple juice, and currant jelly to the pan juices over medium heat. (If you've burned the pan juices, clean the pan out and start over with new butter.)
4. Bring the sauce to a simmer, reduce the heat to low and simmer until the sauce is thickened. (The sauce will have some body rather than just flatten out in the bottom of a spoon.)
5. Return the steaks to the sauce, spoon the simmering sauce over the steaks and let cook another 2 minutes. Serve hot.

## Wild Sides: Oven Fried Potatoes
Serves 4-6
1 pound red potatoes (about 4 medium)
2 tablespoons oil
1 teaspoon garlic salt
1/2 teaspoon coarse black pepper
1 tablespoon dried minced onion flakes
2 tablespoon grated Parmesan cheese
1 to 2 teaspoons kosher salt

Preparation
1. Preheat the oven to 475°F. Cut the potatoes lengthwise, then crosswise, 1/4 inch thick. (In other words, traditional French fry shape.)
2. In a plastic bag, combine the oil, garlic salt, pepper, and dried minced onion. Add the cut fries, and toss until well coated.
3. Generously oil a cookie sheet and spread the fries in a single layer. Place in the oven. At 15 minutes, flip the fries with a spatula, and return to the oven for about 10 more minutes, or until light to golden brown. Transfer to individual plates or a platter and sprinkle with the Parmesan cheese and kosher salt.

Fall-Apart Oven Pot Roast
recipe on page 134

Meredith's Secret Ingredient Stew
recipe on page 142

Pan-Roasted Safari Steaks
recipe on page 84

Slice Of The Wild

Cheatin' Ribs
recipe on page 123

The $5 Solution
instructions on page 103

Stacks of Steaks or Reams of Roasts?
see Custom Cutting for Your Table
pages 43-58

Old World Marinated Venison & Potato Kabobs
&
Wild Side: Grilled Sweet Bells
recipes on pages 72 & 63

Wild Sides: Half-Mashed Potatoes
recipe on page 110

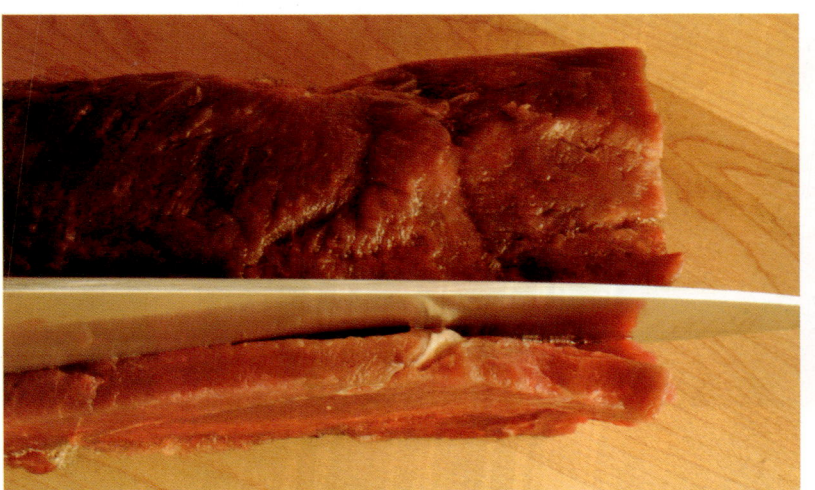

Two Neat Tricks for Cut Meat Jerky
1. Cut the meat while it's frozen.
2. Shake the jerky seasoning mix out of an old spice jar.

Meatballs and Spaghetti
recipe on page 158

Put a Lid On It
(any soup or stew, that is)
recipe on page 138

Wild Sides: Shiitake-Laced Scalloped Potatoes
recipe on page 108

Sautéed Pepper and Onions
recipe on page 78

Wild Sides: Potato Pancakes
recipe on page 169

Easy Tex-Mex Pulled Venison
recipe on page 130

Christmas Chorizo Rollups
recipe on page 116

Brisket In Fire Roasted Red Pepper Sauce
recipe on page 124

94   Slice Of The Wild

Sausage and Jerky
case it or shape into patties
recipes start on page 164

Tex-Mex Potato Salad
recipe on page 71

96 Slice Of The Wild

# The Tender End
## Dry Roasting

# Dry Roasting Made Easy And Predictable

If pot roasts are comfort food, dry-roasted meats are white tie and tails. And while we'll roast both ways on a Saturday morning then feast on the leftovers all weekend, there is some truth in the difference. Why? I always imagine dry roasts as the centerpiece of Sunday afternoon dinner at my Grandma's house. I'm still in my go-to-church dress and my Dad's in his good suit and tie. Formal. Pot roast is for cold, snowy Saturday afternoons when you're layered up in sweats and thick wool socks with the Packers and the Bears on TV--the very definition of comfort.

The other differences in dry vs. wet roasting are the cut you use, the temperature you cook it at, and the desired doneness. In wet roasting you can cook the devil out of the meat, and the slow, moist heat will keep it tender. Try that with higher temperature dry roasting and you'll end up with the proverbial hockey puck. That's true of commercial meats, too. The worst waste of meat I ever saw was an over-cooked beef prime rib that must have cost a fortune and was impossible to chew.

For game meats, the other problem is that the further you push dry-cooked game meats toward well done, the more concentrated the gamy flavors. For the record, dry roasting includes any cooking method that does not include moisture, whether it is water, wine, bouillon or even oil. So, for those who like their venison way past when the pink was gone, please tear out these dry roasting pages and never, ever cook anything this way. Stick to wet. Dry roasting is for those who like their meat between bloody rare and just-barely-past-pink medium, at the very most.

By definition, then, since dry roasting doesn't add moisture or allow for a slow breaking down of tougher cuts, it is best suited for tender parts of the animal, and people who aren't turned off by a little pink or red in the middle. (Doesn't matter if it's wild or domestic, that's when dry-cooked meat is most tender.) Wet cooking, on the other hand, allows for the slow, moist correction of tough cuts, and what could become tough through over-cooking using the dry method. If you like it done well, and don't like it tough, then cook wet. That includes pot roasts, slow cookers, and braising--a combination of browning, the addition of liquid, and at least 45 minutes covered cooking time.

## Grading Your Venison

So what cuts are tender? Whether deer, antelope, cattle, elk, lamb, or caribou, tender is located high and to the rear on any four-legged animal. The higher you go, the further back you go, the more tender the meat should be. Conversely, the lower you go, and the more forward, the tougher an animal can be, relatively. Some venison is tender all over, like spring lamb is tender all over, but mature animals are tender high and back toward the base of the tail, not so tender low on the front quarter. That's why many butchering 'experts' take the safe route and recommend relegating the entire front quarter to burger and, equally, why tenderloins don't last long in the freezer. (But have you noticed the back end of the tenderloin is always more tender than the front?)

There is a simple test to find out just how tough or tender your venison is. I've tucked it in right between field care and butchering because that's the best time to test your animal—before you cut it up. For now, we'll assume you've done the Taste & Tenderness Test, and know what cuts you can cook in this Tender End section of recipes, and what you'll have to turn over to the Tougher End section. Let's get back to cooking.

## Dry Vs. Wet: Choosing the Right Recipe

Wet roasting is the cover and bake sort of meal we associate with briskets and pot roasts. For that, tough cuts like brisket and shoulder roasts are ideal, because they not only need the slow, wet cooking for us to enjoy chewing them, but they'll hold together and not fall apart as a tenderloin would. Not that I haven't seen folks cook perfectly good tenderloins long and slow (or cut them into jerky, for that matter). I've had two animals in my house that were tough enough to warrant that kind of treatment, but the vast majority of tenderloins don't need that much work or energy to taste good.

Then there's your valuable time. Steaks are still the fastest way to get meat on the table, but dry roasting is a pretty fast method of cooking—compared to pot roasting, at least—and more energy efficient in that it brings more ready-to-munch meat to the table with the same effort.

In our house we cook roasts mostly for the leftovers: thinly sliced in sandwiches, with red onion, lettuce, tomato, a little salt and pepper, and a lot of mayonnaise. (I know it's not practical, but I'd like to invite everyone who's ever said cold venison tastes awful to lunch at my house. Cold venison is as good as the hot venison it once was, because if you start with a good-tasting animal and don't mishandle it on the way to the table, it won't magically turn into mutton when it cools.)

## Choosing A Temperature

Once you've decided to dry roast, pick a speed. I prefer roasting at 450°F because I'm always running late. A whitetail tenderloin can be done in less than an hour; a moose slightly over an hour. A big rump roast can be done in less time than it takes to clean Vibram soles. However, a lot of folks don't feel as comfortable with dry roasting and have kids, so dinner time can be hectic and very distracting. For them, dry roasting at 325°F takes longer, but is more forgiving. At 450°F, if you get side-tracked, you can end up with a large, overdone patio paver. At 325°F, you have a little wiggle room on the timer.

## When Will It Be done?

Whichever cooking temperature you choose, keep in mind that the timing is based on the thickness of the roast, not on its overall size or weight. Most of us are used to tables that correlate roasting time and temperature to weight. But those tables refer to beef; except for moose and some bull elk, venison animals simply aren't that large, and in truth, I suspect thickness is a better predictor of cooking time with beef as well. But since game animals and cuts are smaller, and less fatty, proper cooking time is more crucial. It pays to keep a cheap plastic ruler in the knife drawer, and to stand it up behind your roast just before it goes in the oven. Ignore the length. Ignore the weight. Measure the height. Then look at the chart that follows, and set a kitchen timer according to that estimate.

## Telling Time: Some Guidelines

1. Use a meat thermometer. Insert it into the thickest part of the roast, at least 1" deep because on most meat thermometers, there are no sensors at the tip, they're an inch up the shaft.
2. Let the thermometer sit in the meat for 10 minutes: all roasts rise 5 to 7 degrees in temperature the first 8-10 minutes after being removed from the oven. It's not until then that the reading is accurate.
3. If you are cooking a bone-in roast, avoid touching the bone with the meat thermometer. Bones get hotter than meat.
4. Until you know your oven, it's best to underestimate the timing. Start with the chart, then subtract 10 degrees from your ideal 'done' temperature. Then, check the roast with a meat thermometer about two thirds through your estimate. And, always use a timer.
5. Once the roast has reached 100°F internal temperature, it takes approximately a half minute to rise 1 degree more. So check the temperature well before you need to, then recalculate the time to your desired finished temperature. (Add 1 minute for each 2 degrees higher you want it to be. After the internal temperature has reached 100°F, it will be 110° in 5 minutes, 120° in 10, and so on.)

Red rare is 120°; rosy rare is 125°; medium rare 130°; a slightly pink medium 140°: to allow for counter rise, take the roast out 10° before your ideal temperature. Remember, you can always add more cooking time; never subtract it. For those concerned with cooking wild meat as rare as 120°, if you killed and cut it, you know how clean it is. And once you fill in your personal roasting chart, timing will get a lot easier.

One more thing. You'll notice in this roasting section that for some recipes, I'll call for a 2 or 3 pound roast rather than a roast so many inches tall. That's because even though the weight is irrelevant to estimate cooking time, it's still very relevant for estimating how much meat you need for the number of people you're serving. Health experts recommend 1/4 pound of meat per person. While women tend to follow that rule of thumb, men don't. Teenage boys inhale animal protein as easily as air, but I have male friends in their 40's and 50's who sit down to a roast and don't stop eating until it's gone or they're groaning in pain. And of course when I'm hosting dinner I don't want anyone to go home meat hungry. The serving sizes in this book are based on the 1/4 pound per person estimate; adjust them to fit the meat eaters you're serving.

## Venison Roasting Table

I live at almost 4,000 feet above sea level and cook in a propane gas oven, so I've included a blank roasting table on the next page that you can fill in for your oven because my home oven will differ somewhat from yours. Yes, they're all calibrated when installed, but ovens still differ. If you don't feel comfortable writing in a cookbook, copy the blank table and tape it to the inside of a cupboard door.

Each time you roast, use my table as a guideline, but check the roast with a meat thermometer about 2/3 through the estimated time. Then, fill in the details for your oven on your chart. Soon, you'll have an incredibly precise and reliable time table for your oven and grill. (Until you replace them.)

Here are the charts. You'll notice on the upper chart, I've started at 120°F as a finished temperature rather than the 125°F listed in the recipes: it's like setting your watch 5 minutes fast, but this time to allow for that 5° counter rise when estimating cooking time. And if you still end up over-cooking your roast, fix it with the $5 Solution. (Believe me, we've had to use it more than once.)

To start your own personal roasting table, and have the $5 Solution handy in emergencies, turn the page. I've left lots of room on those two pages for you to make your own notes.

### Indoors

*dry roasting table*

| | roast height | rare 120°F | medium 140°F |
|---|---|---|---|
| **325°F oven** | 1 3/4" | 45 min. | 55 min. |
| | 2" | 55 min. | 65 min. |
| | 2 1/2" | 60 min. | 70 min. |
| | 3" | 65 min. | 75 min. |
| **450°F oven** | 1 3/4" | 25 min. | 35 min. |
| | 2" | 30 min. | 40 min. |
| | 2 1/2" | 40 min. | 50 min. |
| | 3" | 50 min. | 60 min. |

### Outdoors

| | roast height | rare 120° | medium 140° |
|---|---|---|---|
| **325°F covered grill** | 2" | 35 min. | 45 min. |
| | 2 1/2" | 45 min. | 55 min. |
| | 3" | 55 min. | 65 min. |

Slice Of The Wild

*your personal dry roasting table*

## Indoors

| roast height | rare 120°F | medium 140°F |
|---|---|---|
| 325°F oven | | |
| 1 1/2" | | |
| 2" | | |
| 2 1/2" | | |
| 3" | | |
| 450°F oven | | |
| 1 1/2" | | |
| 2" | | |
| 2 1/2" | | |
| 3" | | |

## Outdoors

| roast height | rare 120°F | medium 140°F |
|---|---|---|
| 325°F covered grill | | |
| 2" | | |
| 2 1/2" | | |
| 3" | | |

Slice Of The Wild

# The $5 Solution: A Backwards Marinade

I'm not pointing fingers, but sometimes things happen. You don't hear the timer, or forget to set the timer, and suddenly you smell meat, and it's cooked way past the medium rare you planned to serve. Help is here in a grab-what's-handy first aid remedy that works so well you'll find yourself using it in non-emergencies.

You'll need a stand-up $5 Thermos bottle (the half gallon size will fit most game roasts), and a full bottle of salad dressing--your choice. I prefer Brianna's Home Style Zesty French, but any Italian, Catalina, or French dressing will do.

The trick is to remove the roast from the oven and transfer it immediately into the cooler while it's still oven-hot. (I use tongs for small roasts; oven mitts for larger ones. Whatever, use caution and don't get burned.) Then pour the salad dressing into the thermos jug with it and seal the cooler tight. (Yes, pour it in cold. The roast will heat it up.)

Roll the cooler around on the counter for a few minutes. Then let it sit for 10 or 15 minutes more, still sealed up, to let the juices really penetrate the meat. (The oven-hot roast creates a vacuum inside the cooler, and sucks the dressing right up, like a power marinater.) After 15 minutes, remove and enjoy.

If you do start using this method of marinating as a regular thing, you may want to mix up one of the many marinades in this book instead of just popping the cork on a prepared salad dressing. Or not. But do feel free to use the $5 Solution on game birds, too. It works.

## Indirect al Fresco Roast
Serves 6-8

Put the fire on one end of the grill, the roast on the other. Or split the fire and put the roast in the middle. You'll need a covered grill that produces even temperatures whether you're using propane, briquettes, or wood. Bursts of heat that make it hard to predict cooking times will lead to either stressful cooking or culinary disasters. Indirect grilling is all about using the heat, but not letting it sear the roast itself.

### Ingredients
2 pound rump roast, or tenderloin
1/2 cup softened butter
1 tablespoon freshly squeezed lemon juice
1 tablespoon chopped shallots
1 teaspoon salt
1 teaspoon coarse black pepper
2 teaspoons dried leaf tarragon

### Cooking
1. Preheat the grill to 450°. Trim and dry the roast. In one bowl mix together the butter, lemon juice, and shallots until smooth. In a separate bowl, combine the salt, pepper, and tarragon.
2. Cut two long slits the length of the top of the roast, about 1 inch from the ends and 1 inch deep. Fill these two slits with the butter/shallot mixture. Rub the tarragon mixture into the meat.
3. Before starting the roast, measure its height by standing a ruler behind it. A 2-inch tall roast will take about 25 to 35 minutes at 450° for rosy rare (125°F on the meat thermometer). Allow about 1/2 minute for each degree higher you want; about 130°F for medium rare, 140°F for slightly pink medium. Remove the roast from the oven 5°F below your ideal finish to allow for counter rise.
4. To serve: bring the roast to the table hot, or chill and serve with Red Ranch Rotini Salad for cool summer dinners.

****Feel free to substitute fresh tarragon for the dry. Or use another herb mixture: my other favorite is 1 tablespoon each of fresh basil and oregano blended with 2 chopped green onions in 2 tablespoons of butter. Salt and pepper as above.

## Wild Sides: Red Ranch Rotini Salad
Serves 4-6

Make this salad 24 to 48 hours ahead and you'll notice a lot more flavor.

Ingredients
1/2 pound rotini, cooked and drained
2 tomatoes, seeded and diced
2 cups diced cucumber
2 cups diced celery
1 red sweet bell pepper, diced
4 green onions, diced
1/2 cup Red Ranch Dressing (see note)

### Preparation
In a large bowl, combine the chopped vegetables with the rotini, then toss with the Red Ranch Dressing. Chill and serve.

To make Red Ranch Dressing: add 1 tablespoon of mild McCormick Taco Seasoning to an 8 ounce bottle of Ranch Dressing. Shake well.

# Grilled Tenderloin Stuffed with Piggy Salsa
Serves 6

This recipe came from fellow venison lovers, Kay and Bob Avery. Another indirect roast for the grill, it's easy and tasty and adds that delicate fat flavor we all know isn't in low fat venison. It's Kay and Bob's favorite recipe for a very good reason.

## Ingredients
1/2 cup pork breakfast sausage
1/2 cup fresh tomato salsa
10-inch length of tenderloin, trimmed
6 slices bacon

## Cooking
1. Preheat the grill to medium heat (about 325°F). In a bowl, combine the sausage and salsa. Place the tenderloin on a cutting board and with a sharp boning knife, slice it in half, so you have a top and bottom, and lay the top aside. Arrange the bacon slices on the cutting board side by side, and lay the bottom half of the tenderloin on top of them.
2. Spread the sausage/salsa on the bottom half and place the top half on that. Now fold the bacon over the top, and secure it with toothpicks.
3. Wipe a little oil on the bottom of the tenderloin and place it on the grill, but not directly over the fire. Check with a meat thermometer in about 45 minutes: the tenderloin is done when the thermometer registers 165° to 170°F. (The higher temperature is for the bacon and the pork stuffing. All that pork fat will keep the venison more moist than otherwise.) Remove the roast from the grill 5°F below your ideal finish to allow for counter rise.
4. Let the tenderloin sit for 5-7 minutes before slicing it across the grain. Serve with Sweet and Sour Slaw.

****Choose a deer-sized tenderloin (upper piece) or a hanging tenderloin (lower piece) from a moose or elk.

# Wild Sides: Sweet and Sour Slaw
Serves 8

My grandmother's coleslaw may have tasted better, but she spent hours slicing the cabbage precisely thin enough to absorb the perfect amount of dressing. That's more work than most of us are willing to do. Plus Grandma took that recipe to her grave; neither my Mom nor I have ever been able to reproduce it. However, this version is very tasty, and not nearly as much work.

## Ingredients
1 pound bag pre-cut coleslaw mix
1 cup frozen concentrate pineapple juice, thawed
1 cup mayonnaise
1 tablespoon freshly grated ginger

## Preparation
1. Empty the slaw mix bag into a bowl. Combine the juice, mayonnaise, and ginger, and mix thoroughly in a second bowl.
2. When the mayonnaise/ginger mixture is thoroughly mixed, toss it with the slaw. Cover, refrigerate until chilled, and then serve.

****To make this even easier, use the ready-grated ginger that comes in a tube.

# Pancetta Rump
Serves 6-8

Barding, or the laying on of fat, is a very traditional way to make lean meat more moist. We've all barded before, mostly by laying a slice or three of bacon on top of a roast or wrapping it around a steak. Just two ounces of pancetta, Italian bacon which is cured but not smoked, adds a big burst of flavor.

## Ingredients
1 teaspoon dried leaf thyme
1 teaspoon kosher salt
1 teaspoon coarse black pepper
Tender rump roast (about 2 inches high, 8 inches long)
1 tablespoon oil
2 ounces sliced pancetta

## Cooking
1. Preheat the oven to 325°F. Combine the thyme, salt, and pepper in a small bowl. Trim and dry the roast with paper towels.
2. Wipe the oil on the sides and bottom of the roast, then set oil-side down in a roasting pan. Sprinkle the salt mixture on the roast, and pat it into the meat. Arrange the pancetta on the top in a single layer.
3. Before starting the roast, measure its height by standing a ruler behind it. A 1 1/2-inch tall roast will take about 35 to 45 minutes at 325° for rosy rare (125°F on the meat thermometer). Allow about 1/2 minute for each 1 degree higher you want; about 130°F for medium rare, 140°F for slightly pink medium. Remove the roast from the oven 5°F below your ideal finish to allow for counter rise.
4. When done, remove from the oven and let the roast sit 5 minutes before carving. Slice thin, and serve with French style green beans (with a little bit of Tuscan Herbed Butter, melted on top) and these Irish Mashed Potatoes.

# Wild Sides: Irish Mashed Potatoes
Serves 3-4

If you can make mashed potatoes you can make this classic Irish dish. (In Ireland they call it colcannon and don't make it the same way twice.) This is the way I like it, and even though I don't like cooked spinach on its own, sautéing the greens in butter transforms them into melt-in-your-mouth delicious.

## Ingredients
2 pounds red potatoes, quartered
1/4 cup water
6 tablespoons butter, in all
1/4 head of cabbage, cored and sliced thickly
1 cup lightly packed spinach leaves, chopped
2/3 cup milk

## Cooking
1. Boil the potatoes until fork tender, as you would for plain mashed potatoes. While the potatoes cook, add 1/4 cup water and 2 tablespoons of the butter to a large skillet. Bring it to a boil. Add the chopped cabbage and reduce the heat to medium-high. Simmer the cabbage until tender, about 15 minutes. Transfer to a small bowl.
2. In the same skillet on medium heat, melt another tablespoon of butter until it sizzles. Add the chopped spinach. Sauté until just wilted, about 2 minutes. Add the spinach to the cabbage and set aside.
3. When the potatoes are done, drain, and toss them into a large bowl. Add the rest of the butter and enough of the milk to mash the potatoes until smooth. Stir or whip in the cabbage/spinach mixture. (An electric mixer won't hurt the greens at this point.) Serve hot with salt and pepper to taste.

Slice Of The Wild

# Traditional (Well, Sorta) Venison Wellington
Serves 8

Looking for a traditional Wellington? This isn't it. Who has time to make puff pastry or money enough for big beef roasts when they have a freezer full of venison? We will, however have time to sauté the mushrooms in butter; that takes less than 5 minutes and the flavor reward is well worth the effort. Use oyster mushrooms as I did here or your favorites. Just use something with a bit of color and flavor--not the ubiquitous white ones. And forget the dry roasting chart for just this dish: its pastry covering traps heat very effectively, making the roast cook much faster than without it. In fact, cooking time was reduced by a significant one third. For a 2-inch tall roast at 325°F, allow only 30 to 35 minutes instead of the 45 to 50 when un-pastried. Then turn the page for the perfect wild side: Shiitake-Laced Scalloped Potatoes.

## Ingredients
Tenderloin or rump roast, 2-3 pounds
2 tablespoons butter
1/3 cup chopped shallots
2 ounces fresh oyster mushrooms
1/8 teaspoon grated nutmeg
1/4 teaspoon salt
1 package refrigerator crescent rolls
1 egg, beaten

## Cooking
1. Preheat the oven to 325°F. Trim and dry the roast, and let it come to room temperature. In a small skillet, melt the butter over medium heat until it sizzles and just starts to brown, add the shallots and lower the heat to medium-low. Sauté the shallots until golden brown, about 3-4 minutes, then add the mushrooms. Stir the nutmeg and salt into the mushrooms gently, and sauté until they have absorbed all the butter, about 1 minute. Remove the skillet from the heat, and let the mushroom mixture cool.
2. Place the roast in a roasting pan or cast iron skillet large enough so it doesn't touch the sides of the pan. Open the refrigerator crescent rolls, and lay enough out on a piece of waxed paper or plastic wrap to completely cover the roast. (A 3-inch wide by 7-inch long roast will take half the package of rolls.)
3. Pinch and press the seams of the rolls together until they disappear. Spread the mushroom mixture on the top of the roast, then gently drape the crescent roll dough over that. Tuck the excess in under the roast. Brush the crust with the beaten egg, and place the roasting pan in the center of the oven.
4. Roast until a meat thermometer reads 125° for rosy rare, 130° for medium rare, 140° for medium when placed in the thickest part of the roast--right through the crust. Remove the roast from the oven 5°F below your ideal finish to allow for counter rise. Let cool 5 minutes before carving.

# Wild Sides: Shiitake-Laced Scalloped Potatoes
Serves 4-6

I'm 35 miles from the closest place that stocks exotic mushrooms, and never know when the spirit will move me. So I keep a baggy or two of dried exotics in the spice cupboard just in case. This is easy, and makes a big impression at the table.

## Ingredients
1/2 ounce package dried shiitake mushrooms
2 cups milk
3 tablespoons flour
6 potatoes, sliced
4 tablespoons butter or margarine
1 tablespoon dried leaf tarragon
1/2 teaspoon salt
1 teaspoon coarse black pepper

## Preparation
Soak the mushrooms in the milk until tender. About 1-2 hours.

## Cooking
1. Preheat the oven to 350°F. Remove the mushrooms from the milk and slice thin. Stir the flour into the milk, and whip until the lumps are gone.
2. In a 9-inch square baking pan (or 9-inch cast iron skillet), layer the sliced potatoes and butter in two layers, pouring half the milk mixture over each layer. When layered, add a bit more milk if necessary so you can see it between the slices. (It shouldn't cover the potatoes completely, though.)
3. Sprinkle the sliced mushrooms, tarragon, salt, and pepper over the top and cover tightly with foil. Bake 30 minutes covered, then remove the foil and bake another 15 minutes uncovered. Serve hot.

# Easy Pesto Wellington
Serves 8

The previous Wellington doesn't take any liberties. Drenched in prepared basil pesto, this one cuts across cultural boundaries. It's still golden brown and beautiful to look at, and traps moisture for a delicate, juicy roast, but it surprises as well. (The crust also traps heat; making the cooking time about 1/3 what the venison roasting chart says.) Use a good, tender rump roast or a length of tenderloin. Either will make a great company-for-supper dish. And feel free to substitute your own homemade pesto, if you have it.

## Ingredients
8-9 inch length of tenderloin or rump roast (about 2-3 pounds)
1/2 cup prepared basil pesto
1 package refrigerator crescent rolls
1 egg yolk, beaten
Kosher salt

## Cooking
1. Preheat the oven to 325°F. Trim and dry the roast with paper towels, and place it in a heavy-bottomed roasting pan or cast iron skillet large enough not to touch the roast. Spread the pesto on top of the roast.
2. Lay the crescent roll dough on a sheet of wax paper or plastic wrap and pinch the seams together; place over the roast. Tuck, and pinch the dough so it fits snugly around the roast.
3. Brush the crescent dough with beaten yolk, and sprinkle with a teaspoon of kosher salt. Place the roast in the oven. For a 3-inch tall roast, cook about 45 minutes until a meat thermometer in the thickest part reads 120° for rosy rare, 130° for medium rare, 140° for medium. (Yes, through the crust.) Remove the roast from the oven 5°F below your ideal finish to allow for counter rise.
4. When done, let the roast sit for 5 minutes, then carve, and serve. Since the salt content of pesto varies, whether homemade or bottled, add more kosher salt at the table to taste.
****Choose a rump or a deer-sized tenderloin (upper piece) or a hanging tenderloin (lower piece) from a moose or elk.

# Wild Sides: Roasted Veggies
Serves 4

A perfect winter dish that goes with roasts, steaks and burgers. All the vegetables are sliced into spears--the length of the vegetable--in about equal thickness so it all cooks at the same rate. Wait until you see how rich and satisfying a dish this simple can be.

## Ingredients
4 medium potatoes, quartered lengthwise
1 pound carrots, peeled and halved
1 medium yellow onion, in eighths
2 tablespoons dried onion flakes
1 teaspoon salt
1 teaspoon pepper
1/4 cup oil

## Cooking
1. Preheat the oven to 475°F. Toss the veggies into a plastic bag; add the onion flakes, salt, and pepper to the oil in a measuring cup, then pour the mixture over the vegetables. Close the bag tightly and shake to coat.
2. Arrange the veggies on two lightly oiled 9x13 baking sheets, in a single layer, and place in the center of the oven, uncovered. Roast for 45 to 50 minutes, turning them twice with a spatula. Serve while hot.
*Cook's Note: for a really sweet variation, add a sliced rutabaga (sliced about 1/8-inch thick). Roasted, they're about as sweet as the carrots, and are a nice surprise on a cold winter's night.

## Spike: The Larded Roast
Serves 6-8

Larding a roast is slightly different that barding it. With barding, you lay the bacon on top; in larding, you poke the fat into the meat. It will take a few minutes longer, but the flavor and fat gets way inside the meat. You can use any fat; but cured pork--bacon, Italian ham--is the most common. And, if you've got too much on your plate already--pun intended--just lay the bacon on top. The effect will be close enough. If the roast is gamy, poke peeled garlic cloves into the holes along with the bacon strips.

### Ingredients
Rump or tenderloin roast, about 2-3 pounds
3 slices bacon
3 tablespoons barbecue sauce

### Cooking
1. Preheat the oven to 325°F. Trim and dry the roast. Set in a heavy-bottomed roasting pan or cast iron skillet large enough so it doesn't touch the sides. Slice 2 pieces of bacon in half lengthwise, and into 2-3" lengths. Pour the barbecue sauce onto a plate, and dredge the bacon through it.
2. With a sharp paring knife, poke holes in the roast, but don't pierce the bottom. (You want the fat to bubble through the roast as it cooks, not seep out.) Now with a spoon handle, stuff the bacon into the holes. Cut the last slice of bacon into three pieces and lay them across the top of the roast.
3. Before starting the roast, measure its height by standing a ruler behind it. A 2-inch tall roast will take about 45 to 55 minutes at 325° for rosy rare (125°F on the meat thermometer). Allow about 1/2 minute for each degree higher you want; about 130°F for medium rare, 140°F for slightly pink medium. Remove the roast from the oven 5°F below your ideal finish to allow for counter rise.

****Choose a rump roast or a deer-sized tenderloin (upper piece) or a hanging tenderloin (lower piece) from a moose or elk.

## Half-Mashed Potatoes
Serves 4-6

My Grandmother made the whippiest, smoothest mashed potatoes on the Eastern seaboard. Apparently, in her day, texture was the thing. These half-mashed aren't quite as creamy, but the flavor has been ramped up a bunch, so if you leave a lump or two no one will notice.

### Ingredients
1 pound white or red potatoes
1 softball-sized rutabaga
1/2 cup milk
1/2 cup sour cream
3 tablespoons butter or margarine
1 teaspoon salt
1/2 teaspoon pepper

### Cooking
1. Quarter the potato and rutabaga, cover with cold water, put the lid on top, and bring to a boil. Cook until the rutabaga is fork tender. Drain the cooking liquid and transfer the veggies to a large bowl.
2. Mash or whip the potatoes, adding the milk, sour cream, and butter gradually. Salt, pepper, and serve.

Slice Of The Wild

# Succulent Roast Tenderloin
Serves 4 to 6

The last time I made this roast, I used a tenderloin from an adult whitetail buck. (The upper tender piece.) His tenderloin was 3 1/2 inches wide, by 2 1/4 inches high, and almost 2 feet long. I cut a 9-inch length, perfect for my husband and me, with leftovers. But the recipe is expandable if you refer to the time vs. height table at the beginning of this chapter. Remember, it's the height, not the weight that counts. Keep a cheap plastic ruler with your kitchen knives and you can adjust this recipe for an elk or moose tenderloin--or any other tender roast on any animal--for any roast recipe in this book.

## Ingredients
3 tablespoons softened butter
3 tablespoons Dijon mustard
9-10 inch length of whitetail tenderloin
1 teaspoon coarse ground black pepper

## Cooking
1. Preheat the oven to 450°F. In a small bowl combine the butter and mustard into a soft paste. Dry the tenderloin with paper towels and place in a roasting pan.
2. With a table knife, spread the butter/mustard paste across the top of the tenderloin. Sprinkle with the pepper.
3. Before starting the roast, measure its height by standing a ruler behind it. A 2-inch tall roast will take about 25 to 30 minutes at 450° to reach 125° for rosy rare; allow 1/2 minute for each degree more of doneness (130° for medium rare; 140° for medium). Remove the roast from the oven 5°F below your ideal finish to allow for counter rise.
4. Let sit 5 minutes before carving, then slice thick or thin. Spoon the pan drippings over the slices and serve.

****Choose a deer-sized tenderloin (upper piece) or a hanging tenderloin (lower piece) from a moose or elk.

# Wild Sides: Savory Rice
Serves 4-6

I love the earthy, deep, belly-warming flavor of this rice. Combining the tarragon, balsamic vinegar and Worcestershire sauce somehow makes each ingredient taste even better than they would have tasted separately.

## Ingredients
4 tablespoons butter
4 tablespoons fresh tarragon, minced
1 medium yellow onion, sliced thin
1/4 cup balsamic vinegar
1 cup uncooked rice
2 cups beef broth
2 cups water
1/2 teaspoon black pepper

## Cooking
1. In a saucepan, melt the butter over medium heat until it starts to brown slightly. Add the tarragon and onion, and sauté the onion until soft, about 4-5 minutes. Add the balsamic vinegar and continue cooking until the vinegar is almost gone.
2. Add the rice, stir it into the onion mixture, and sauté another 1-2 minutes until the rice starts to brown. Add the broth, water, and pepper, raise the heat to high, and bring to a low simmer. Cover, reduce the heat to low, and cook until the water is absorbed, about 40 minutes. (There will be 'eyes' or dimples in the surface of the rice when it's done.) Serve hot.

# Gideon's Grub Rub Goes A-Roasting

John and I have a theory. It isn't just the melt-in-your-mouth fat that some folks miss when they call game meat 'gamy' but it's the sweetness that commercially raised meat fat gives to the meat. Before the diet police made restaurants cut off all the fat from our beef steaks, that was what we liked best about dining out. Me, too. Our theory goes further. We find that spice mixes made for commercial meat just don't work as well on game because they assume the sweet will be in the meat. And with game, it's not. That's why bacon is such a popular ingredient with game, and why Gideon's Grub Rub also works. It has sugar in it, and turns this simple rub mixture into a cure-all. (If you want to really go crazy, substitute butter for the oil.) For convenience sake, I've repeated the Grub Rub recipe below.)

## Ingredients

2 pound rump roast
2 tablespoons brown sugar
1 tablespoon oil
Salt to taste

## Cooking

1. Preheat the oven to 450°F. In a small bowl combine the oil, brown sugar and Grub Rub into a soft paste. Dry the roast with paper towels.
2. With a table knife, spread the brown sugar/Rub paste across the top of the roast.
3. Before starting the roast, measure its height by standing a ruler behind it. A 2-inch tall roast will take about 25 to 30 minutes at 450° to reach 120° for rosy rare; allow 1/2 minute for each degree more of doneness (130° for medium rare; 140° for medium). Remove the roast from the oven 5°F below your ideal finish to allow for counter rise.
4. Let sit 5 minutes before carving, then slice thick or thin. Spoon the pan drippings over the slices and serve.

## Gideon's Grub Rub

1/2 cup salt
1 1/2 teaspoons MSG
1 tablespoon coarse ground black pepper
2 tablespoons white sugar
1 tablespoon sweet paprika
3 tablespoons dried onion flakes
1 teaspoon garlic power
Combine in a glass jar, shake, and cover until dinner time.

# The Middle
## Ribs, Brisket & Flank Steaks

# Tasty and Tender Oven Bag Flank Steaks
Serves 4

Oven bags come in two varieties: foil and plastic. They both vastly decrease the time necessary to tenderize meat, but if you use the plastic one, only poke one hole in the bag. That's enough. As for the salsa, if you don't have access to fresh, and don't have the ingredients or inclination to make your own, buy a can or two of Rotel. It's as close to fresh as a canned jalapeno pepper and tomato mixture can be. Pheasant, chukar and Hungarian partridge are also good prepared this way, with any of the sauces in this section, as are turkey legs, so don't limit the sauced oven bag to red meat.

## Ingredients
1 large foil oven bag
1 cup sour cream
1 cup fresh salsa
1/2 cup beef bouillon (to make it slightly runny)
1 pound flank steaks

## Cooking
1. Preheat the oven to 300°F. Prepare the foil oven bag per package directions. Combine the salsa, sour cream, and bouillon in a small bowl, then pour 1/3 of the mixture into the oven bag. Set the steaks on the sauce in a single layer, then pour the rest of the salsa/sour cream over them. Seal the oven bag as per package directions.
2. Place in a roasting pan or dish at least 1 inch deep, place in the center of the oven, and bake for 90 minutes. Transfer the steaks from the bag to a platter, and pour the cooking sauce over all. Serve with Tex-Mex Potato Salad or Super Creamy Mac & Cheese. (Substitute Monterey Jack for the mozzarella and Parmesan cheeses if you want.)

\*\*\*\*The only trick to this recipe is to have enough sauce to almost cover the meat. If one cup of each isn't enough, mix more.

# Wild Sides: Kool, Keen Quinoa Salad

My baby brother brought the fixings for this great hot weather dish when he came fishing last year. Pronounced keen-wa, quinoa is a whole grain that cooks in a matter of minutes, so it won't heat up the kitchen, but it will spark your appetite.

## Ingredients
1 cup quinoa, raw
2 cups water
2 cups chopped spinach
6 ounce bag dried cranberries
3/4 cup chopped pecans
3/4 cup chopped celery
1/2 cup chopped red onion
6 green onions, chopped
4 lemons
1/4 cup olive oil
1/4 cup mayonnaise

## Preparation
1. Cook the quinoa according to package directions.
2. While the quinoa cools, measure the spinach, cranberries, pecans, celery, red and green onions into a large bowl.
3. Squeeze the lemons, and combine in a small bowl with the oil. Whip until slightly frothy, and then stir in the mayonnaise.
4. Add the quinoa and dressing to the chopped veggies and gently toss. Chill and serve.

# Flank Steak Fajitas
Serves 4-6

Deer and antelope-sized animals don't have as thick a brisket as elk and moose do for corning or braising so most people take that thin strip of meat lying along the rib cage and grind it into burger. But it can also make a fantastic grilled fajita--if you marinate it 36-48 hours. If you don't have brisket or flank or skirt steaks, any steak will do.

## Ingredients
2 tablespoons apple cider vinegar
2 tablespoons oil
2 teaspoons chipotle adobo sauce
1/4 cup freshly squeezed orange juice
Juice of one lime, about 1/4 cup
1 tablespoon honey
1/2 cup sweet onion, chopped
3 cloves garlic, minced
1 teaspoon ground cumin
1 teaspoon chili powder
1/2 teaspoon salt
1/4 teaspoon white pepper
1 tablespoon smoked chipotle Tabasco sauce
1 1/2 to 2 pounds flank steak
6-8 flour tortillas
Fresh salsa
Lettuce
Sour cream

## Preparation
Puree the vinegar, oil, adobo sauce, juices, honey, onion, garlic, cumin, chili powder, salt, white pepper and chipotle Tabasco sauce in a blender. Pour into a resealable plastic bag, add the meat, and seal the bag. Marinate for 2-4 days in the refrigerator, turning the bag once each day. The longer you can marinate this, the better the flavor and tenderness.

## Cooking
1. Preheat the grill to medium-hot. Pour the marinade off, and lay the steaks on the grill. Cook until rare to medium rare, about 10 minutes for 3/4-inch thick steaks.
2. Remove from the grill and slice thin across the grain. Stack on a warmed flour tortilla with fresh salsa, lettuce, and sour cream.
3. Alternately, slice up an onions and a red sweet bell pepper, brush them with the marinade and grill atop a length of foil; roll into the tortilla with the flank steak.

# Christmas Chorizo Rollups
Serves 4

Marinate a pound of flank steaks, then wrap them around some chorizo from the sausage section of this book, and you'll find yourself with a delicious, easy dinner that can double as a fancy entrée some evening when you have more company than time. Flank comes off the outside of the rib cage; on bigger animals it's the thinner end of the brisket. But on smaller animals the brisket is as thin as flank steak so there's no reason not to cook it as flank steak. (Take the best of what's hanging on the rib cage for flank; the rest can still be burger.) You can also use a piece of moderately tender steak, sliced 1/4 to 3/8-inch thick. (Cut them thin, or pound them thin.) The marinade will do the rest. Flank steaks aren't always tough, but it never hurts to marinate them for flavor.

## Ingredients
1 pound flank steaks
1/4 cup rice wine vinegar
1/2 cup oil
3 cloves garlic, minced
1/4 cup minced fresh cilantro
1/2 teaspoon salt
1/4 teaspoon pepper
1 pound chorizo sausage

## Preparation
1. Dry the flank steaks, and slice into 2 to 2 1/2-inch wide strips, about 6-inches long.
2. Measure the vinegar, oil, garlic, cilantro, salt, and pepper into a resealable plastic bag. Add the steaks, seal the bag and give it a good shake to coat the steaks. Marinate in the refrigerator 48 hours.

## Cooking
1. Preheat the oven to 350°F. Remove the steaks from the marinade, but save the marinade.
2. In a lightly oiled roasting pan, assemble the rollups. Lay out each strip of flank steak, spread the sausage over each, then fold and clasp together with toothpicks. Stand the rollup upright in the pan.
3. Roast 40-50 minutes, until a meat thermometer inserted into the sausage registers 160°F. As the steaks near finishing, take 2 tablespoons of the pan drippings, pour them into a small saucepan, and add the marinade. Bring the sauce to a low boil over high heat, lower the heat to a simmer, and simmer 4 minutes. (Don't skimp on the 4 minutes.) Serve the rollups hot with pan juices poured over the top. And the side? Savory Pasta, Mexican Rice, or Red Ranch Rotini Salad.

# Bloody Mary Brisket
Serves 6-8

Again, as with the braised brisket above, use a large foil oven baking bag, like Reynolds Hot Bags. They are much better at sealing in juices--and making game meats more moist--than the plastic bags with their vent holes. As with the previous recipe, if you don't have a brisket in the freezer use another cut, like the rolled roast you took off the shoulder blade. Just take the string off before cooking.

## Ingredients
1 large foil oven bag
2 cups sour cream
2 cups mild bottled Bloody Mary mix
1.5 ounce packet McCormick's mild Taco Seasoning mix
2 pound brisket

## Cooking
1. Preheat the oven to 300°F. Arrange the foil oven bag in a large roasting pan with the opening tipped up.
2. In a large bowl, combine the sour cream, Bloody Mary mix, and Taco Seasoning mix. Stir well.
3. Pour about 1/3 of the sour cream mixture into the Hot Bag. Add the brisket, and pour the rest of the sour cream mixture over it. Seal the bag shut.
4. Bake in the oven until the brisket is tender, about 3 hours. Slice thin, arrange on the plate with egg noodles, and spoon the sauce on top.

****I use the mild taco seasoning mixes; but if you pour tabasco sauce on everything from scrambled eggs to burritos, use the hot taco spice mix.

# Wild Sides: Chipotle Slaw
Serves 6-8

My grandmother used to slice and dice the cabbage and made a great slaw, but I simply don't have the time. I can make any flavor slaw I want in five minutes with a bag of pre-sliced slaw, adapting it to whatever I'm cooking. This one goes great with a Tex-Mex dinner, or in place of sweet pickle relish when you put your dogs in a bun.

## Ingredients
1 pound bag coleslaw mix
1 cup mayonnaise
Juice of 2 limes (about 1/2 cup)
1 tablespoon sugar
1 tablespoon chipotle Tabasco Sauce

## Preparation
Combine the mayo, lime juice, sugar and chipotle sauce in small bowl. Pour it over the slaw mixture, and stir. Cover and refrigerate at least 3-4 hours.

# Dry Rub Brisket
Serves 6

 The last time I made this brisket recipe, I sliced up the finished brisket and sealed it in a Food Saver vacuum bag (just sealed, not vacuumed) and brought it along on a camping trip. That night, I dropped it into a pot of boiling water, and poured it over pasta, with lots of Parmesan cheese. You can also make hot sandwiches, sliced brisket on garlic bread with lots of sauce, and Parmesan cheese. Because this is such a rich tomato sauce that cooks so long, avoid using cast iron (unless it's enamel-coated), aluminum or any other reactive cooking pot. It will throw the taste off. Teflon works, as does a plastic oven bag.

## Ingredients
The Rub
2 pound brisket
2 tablespoons brown sugar
1 tablespoon kosher salt
1 tablespoon dried onion flakes
1 tablespoon sweet paprika
1/2 teaspoon white pepper
1/2 teaspoon dry mustard
The Rest
3 slices bacon, chopped (about 1 cup)
1 red onion, sliced
1 (6 ounce) can tomato paste
2 cups water
2 cups beef bouillon

## Preparation
1. Trim the brisket, removing fat and rough ends, then dry with paper towels. Combine the dry rub ingredients.
2. Rub the brisket all over with the dry rub, then place in a resealable plastic bag and let the brisket marinate in the refrigerator 24 to 48 hours.

## Cooking
1. Preheat the oven to 350°F. In a 3-quart enamel-coated Dutch oven (or other non-reactive pot) cook the bacon until lightly browned, then add the onion. When the onion is soft, add the brisket, and brown it on two sides (it won't get very brown because of the rub), about 3-4 minutes a side.
2. Combine the tomato paste, water and beef bouillon in a large bowl. Stir until the paste is dissolved, then pour over the brisket. Cover and transfer to the oven. Cook 3 hours, or until tender. Slice thin, and serve over pasta, or on garlic toast for a hot sandwich.

# Sweet and Zingy Brisket
Serves 6

When you're done marinating the brisket, don't throw the marinade away. It forms the base of the cooking sauce, too.

## Ingredients
1 1/2 cup orange juice, in all
1 tablespoon onion flakes
2 tablespoons Hoisin sauce
1 tablespoon sugar
1/2 teaspoon red pepper flakes
1/2 teaspoon garlic powder
2 pound brisket
3 slices side pork, chopped (about 1 cup)
1 cup orange juice
2 cups beef bouillon
1 pound baby carrots

## Preparation
1. Combine 1/2 cup of the orange juice with the onion flakes, Hoisin sauce, sugar, red pepper flakes, and garlic powder in a resealable plastic bag. Add the meat, refrigerate, and let marinate 24 to 48 hours.
2. When you're ready to brown the brisket, pull it out of the bag, but don't dry it, and don't toss the marinade.

## Cooking
1. Preheat the oven to 350°F. In a 3-quart Dutch oven, lightly brown the side pork, then add the brisket and brown it lightly, about 4 minutes a side.
2. Add the bouillon and the rest of the orange juice to the marinade and pour it over the browned brisket. Add the carrots, cover the pot, and transfer to the oven. Cook for 2-3 hours or until tender. (Check the liquid level after 2 hours, and add water if needed.) Slice and serve over rice.

## Wild Sides: Chilled Broccoli Salad
This one is from the kitchen of Andrea and Kurt Nelson. Until his recent retirement, Kurt has been the marketing manager for Redding Reloading Equipment, and it turns out, a great cook who works hard to stay in shape and eat well. His wife, Andrea, had this salad and barbecued chicken waiting for us after a 3-day (successful) turkey hunt.

### Ingredients
1 pound bag broccoli slaw mix (12 ounces)
2 cups chopped celery
2 cups red and green grapes, coarsely chopped
3 green onions, chopped
2-3 tablespoons Bac-Os
2-3 ounces toasted, slivered almonds
1 1/2 cups mayonnaise
2 tablespoons white vinegar
2/3 cup sugar

### Preparation
Throw everything into a large bowl, stir, and chill.

# Corned Brisket

Serves 6-8

True brisket is the flap of meat that lies across the sternum and rib cage, insulating the heart/lung area. Unfortunately, the best briskets, the ones large enough to make a satisfyingly plump corned brisket, are animals the size of elk and moose and a few larger deer. But, in years when we have had a plethora of deer-sized animals in the freezer--and nothing bigger--I've corned shoulder roasts. The grain isn't quite as large as in the bigger animals, but it still makes for a very tasty St. Patty's Day feast, or just a tasty year round sandwich meat. (The water buffalo brisket John brought home while testing bullets with Charlie Sisk in Texas made a mouth-watering corned brisket as well.) Use what you have. The corning will take care of the rest.

## Brine Ingredients
1 1/3 cups Morton's Tender Quick
1 teaspoon black peppercorns
1 teaspoon whole cloves
2 bay leaves
2 teaspoons mixed pickling spices
3 quarts cold water, in all
3-4 pound roast or brisket, 2-3 inches thick

## To Brine
1. Combine the Tender Quick and spices with 1 quart hot water in a jar. Close the jar tightly. Keep it on the counter, shaking every 3-4 minutes until the salt has dissolved.
2. Once the mixture is room temperature, pour it into a five-quart crock. Stir well.
3. Submerge the meat in the brine, adding enough more cold water to cover the meat when you push it down. Press the meat down with a small plate (it will float if you let it), then lay a piece of plastic wrap on the brine's surface. Place on the bottom shelf of the refrigerator.
4. Let the brisket corn in the crock for 2 weeks, rotating the meat top to bottom every few days. In two weeks, remove the meat, pour off the brine, and proceed to cooking. Alternatively, freeze until you're ready to cook it, up to 3 weeks.

## Cooking Ingredients
1 large yellow onion, chopped
1/2 cup malt vinegar
1 can (14.9 ounces) Guinness Stout
1 1/2 teaspoons whole mustard seed
1 1/2 teaspoons whole coriander seed
3/4 teaspoon whole black peppercorns
3/4 teaspoon while dill seed
3/4 teaspoon whole allspice
1 bay leaf
1 pound carrots, peeled and halved
2 pounds potatoes, peeled
1 cabbage, in eighths

## To Cook
1. Place the corned brisket in a five-quart pot. Add enough cold water to cover the meat, and bring to a boil over high heat. Reduce to a simmer and skim any foam from the top of the water. Do not change the water.
2. Add the onion, malt vinegar, Guinness and cooking spices. Cover and simmer for three to four hours or until tender.
3. Add the carrots and potatoes 45 minutes before you want to eat; slip the cabbage wedges under the lid for the last 15 minutes of cooking.
4. To serve: slice the brisket across the grain, arrange the carrots, cabbage and potatoes around the brisket, and serve with mustard.

*Slice Of The Wild*

# Carolina-Style Brisket
Serves 8-10

We use the term 'barbecue' to casually refer to the thing we grill with but that's a misnomer. Grilling is hot and fast, and dry; barbecuing is slow, low, and sometimes moist. This is barbecue, with a 'mop' (a sauce that bastes the meat while cooking) to add even more moisture--and flavor. And, this is my favorite type of barbecue: full of vinegar, tart, tangy, and with a hint of sugar to keep it from going over the edge. With the Two-Can Baked Beans, however, edge is what you'll get. Edge and attitude.

## Ingredients
4 pound brisket
1 teaspoon salt
3 teaspoons black pepper
1 cup apple cider vinegar
2 teaspoons red pepper Tabasco sauce
2 teaspoons sugar

## Preparation
1. Trim the brisket and dry with paper towels. Combine 1 teaspoon of the salt and 1 teaspoon of the pepper, and rub it into the meat. Set aside.
2. In a small bowl, combine the cider vinegar, Tabasco sauce, sugar, and the rest of the salt and pepper. Stir until the solids dissolve.

## Cooking
1. In a kettle grill, start 30 charcoal briquettes. In 25-30 minutes, when the coals are ashy, divide the coals in half and nestle a drip pan the size of the brisket into the middle of the coals. Fill the drip pan 1-inch deep with water. Now check your heat. You should be able to hold your palm at cooking level for about 7 seconds--a low fire. Adjust as needed.
2. Lightly oil the brisket, and place it on the cooking rack directly over the drip pan. Brush with the vinegar/tabasco sauce, and cover the grill. Cook for 2-3 hours, brushing with the sauce every 30 minutes, and replenish the coals and water as needed. (Add about 1/3 new coals each hour; don't let the water dry out.)
3. Serve with Two-Can Baked Beans, or slice thin and pile high on deli rolls. (Mix another batch of the cooking sauce to drizzle over the sandwich and/or spread with Chipotle Slaw.)

# Wild Sides: Two-Can Baked Beans
Serves 6

Actually, these aren't baked beans. They're slow cooked. But started from a couple of cans of Van Camp pork and beans, and jazzed up, they're very tasty and incredibly easy. If that's cheating, wait until you taste what can happen when you add a few common ingredients to an old standby.

## Ingredients
2 cans (15 ounces each) Van Camp pork and beans
1/2 cup Kraft Catalina salad dressing
1 cup French's prepared yellow mustard
6 slices raw bacon, chopped
1 medium yellow onion, chopped
1/4 cup maple syrup
2 tablespoons molasses

## Cooking
In a slow cooker, combine all the ingredients, turn on high and cook for one hour. Now, turn the cooker down to low and let the beans cook 6-8 hours. Serve hot.

# Tipsy Brisket
Serves 6-8

This is a perfect dish for the water smoker, but you can also use a charcoal barbecue, or even propane as long as you can power it down to--and keep consistently at--250°F. Without a water smoker, you'll be cooking indirectly: just light the fire and split it, nestling an aluminum baking dish in the midst of the coals with at least one quart of water in it. Then cook the brisket over the water pan, and replenish the water as needed. If you don't have brisket, feel free to substitute a similarly-sized roast.

## Ingredients
4 hickory wood chunks, 3-4 inches thick
2-3 pound piece of elk or moose brisket
2 teaspoons salt
1 teaspoon pepper
3/4 teaspoon ground ginger

## Sauce
1/3 cup Madeira
1 tablespoon Worcestershire sauce
2 tablespoons vegetable oil
1 tablespoon red wine vinegar
1/2 teaspoon dry mustard
1 tablespoon brown sugar
2 teaspoons onion powder

## Cooking
1. Two hours before you start cooking, cover the wood chunks with water and let them soak.
2. Trim the fat from the brisket and dry with paper towels. Combine the salt, pepper, and ginger in a small bowl and rub over the surface of the meat. Combine the sauce ingredients in a small bowl and set aside.
3. Ready the water smoker; fill the reservoir and add the drained wood chunks as you assemble it.
4. Lightly oil the brisket. Place the brisket on the water smoker and brush with the sauce.
5. Cover and cook for 2-3 hours, or until the meat is very tender, brushing with the sauce each half hour. Do not turn the brisket.
6. Slice thin, and serve with Country Style Potato Salad, or make into sandwiches with a dollop of Red Ranch Dressing. (Red Ranch Dressing: add 1 tablespoon of mild McCormick Taco Seasoning mix to an 8 ounce bottle of ranch dressing. Shake well.)

# Cheatin' Ribs
Serves 6-8

If you're new to ribs, or just like to keep things simple, this is the recipe for you. Choose a tomato-based barbecue sauce, but one with little if any smoke flavor. (The smoke will only intensify in the roasting and may get too strong.) Then just sit back and let the roaster do its stuff. As for the beer, the most common ones, like Miller Genuine Draft, work very well.

## Ingredients
- 2 tablespoons oil
- 2-3 pounds moose or elk ribs, in sections
- 1-2 pounds pork ribs
- 2 12 ounce cans of beer
- 12 ounces of your favorite tomato-based barbecue sauce

## Cooking
1. Preheat the oven to 300°F. Separate the elk/moose ribs and dry with paper towels. Arrange them in the roasting pan, so they make an even layer.
2. In a large skillet, brown the pork ribs in the oil over medium heat until just golden. Transfer them to the roasting pan, covering the game ribs.
3. In a large bowl, combine the beer and barbecue sauce; two 12 ounce beer bottles, with 1 1/2 cups (also 12 ounces) barbecue sauce. Pour over the ribs. (If you need more liquid to cover, mix more.)
4. Cover the roasting pan and roast the ribs 2-3 hours or until tender.

\*\*\*\*Since prepared barbecue sauces vary in salt and pepper content, it's best to not add any salt and pepper to the cooking sauce. Taste the ribs when they're done, and then you can add salt and pepper to taste at the table.

## Need More Rib Recipes?
Use this cover & bake method, or an oven bag, as in the Fire Roasted Brisket, then substitute the cooking sauce from Bloody Mary, Brisket-In-A-Bag, Fire Roasted Pepper Sauce, or the Sneaky Hot Ginger Brisket. Just be sure to keep the proportions the same: about 3 pounds of ribs to 4 cups liquid for a turkey roasting pan, and about half that much liquid for an oven bag. And you can always stretch the sauce with a little beef bouillon if you're a little short.

## Tips & Tactics: Better Ribs
The trick to cooking ribs is first to have enough meat on the ribs to make cooking worthwhile. A trophy deer--whitetail or mule deer--or any moose or elk will provide lots of meat to gnaw on. (Does and young forkhorn deer simply don't have the padding.) However, you can pad the ribs by leaving the brisket and any other flank meat on that big buck, rather than boning it off for the burger pile. Elk and moose, have lots of meat on the ribs without having to do it. But you still can.

The second thing is to saw the ribs into manageable lengths when you're butchering--say, something that will fit into your turkey roasting pan. Sawing them by hand takes time, but doesn't strew quite as much bone dust around as a power band saw. Aside from blood, guts, and hair nothing makes meat gamier than bone dust. So saw them very carefully, then rinse any bone dust off before wrapping and freezing them.

# Brisket in Fire Roasted Red Pepper Sauce
Serves 6-8

It says brisket at the head of this recipe, but you can tuck ribs into the oven bag just as easily--or a rolled shoulder roast. There is plenty of red pepper sauce and it's delicious no matter what you cook in it. Between the sauce and the oven bag tough has no choice but to loosen up.

## Ingredients
2 to 4 pound brisket
4 tablespoons oil, in all
1 onion, chopped
2 fire roasted red peppers (in a bottle)
15 ounce can chopped tomatoes
1 tablespoon molasses
1/4 cup raisins
1/4 teaspoon salt
1/4 teaspoon pepper

## Cooking
1. Preheat the oven to 300°F. Prepare the oven bag: open and set it out in a roasting pan.
2. In a heavy skillet, brown the brisket in 2 tablespoons of the oil over medium heat, until golden brown, about 4-7 minutes. Transfer the brisket to the oven bag.
3. Add the rest of the oil to the skillet and sauté the onion until tender. Add the rest of the ingredients and lower the heat to a simmer. Simmer about 5 minutes, then pour over the brisket in the oven bag. Close the bag, making only one slit in the oven bag, to preserve the moisture for the meat.
4. Bake 2-3 hours, until tender. Slice thin, and serve with Four Bean Salad or Super Creamy Mac & Cheese.

****Roasting gives sweet red bell peppers a genuine tang and if you can't find 'fire roasted' peppers, the more common 'roasted red pepper' will work just as well. They'll be near the bottled pepperoncini peppers in the grocery store.

*tougher ◇ rib or brisket ◇ oven bag*

# Sneaky Hot Ginger Brisket
Serves 4-6

All these cooking sauces for briskets can be turned around and used on ribs as well as roasts too tough for dry roasting. The principle is the same in each recipe: put the tough meat into an oven bag, pour some tasty liquid over it, and slow cook until tender. The oven bag speeds up the process and keeps the kitchen mess to a minimum as well. The other thing that makes life easier is to buy ginger already grated in a tube: it's in the fresh produce section of the grocery store. But do beware. Ginger is hot. This recipe, as written, compares to chili with lots of Tabasco sauce. (Omit the red pepper flakes for a milder flavor.)

## Ingredients
2-4 pound brisket
2 tablespoons oil
1/2 cup apricot nectar
1/2 cup jellied cranberry sauce
2 tablespoons tube or grated ginger
1 teaspoon Worcestershire sauce
1/4 teaspoon red pepper flakes

## Cooking
1. Preheat the oven to 300°F. Prepare the oven bag: open and set it in a roasting pan.
2. In a heavy skillet, brown the brisket in the oil over medium heat, until golden brown, about 4-7 minutes. Transfer the brisket to the oven bag. Make only one slit in the oven bag, to preserve the moisture for the meat.
3. Combine the rest of the ingredients and pour over the brisket. Close the bag, place in the center of the oven, and bake 2-3 hours or until tender.
4. Slice thin and serve on hard rolls, or sliced thick with Traditional Potato Salad and Scalloped Pineapple.

# Braised Brisket-in-a-Bag
Serves 4-6

This is a rich, flavorful brisket recipe, but if you weren't lucky enough to get a moose or elk this year--or a big, healthy buck--the recipe also works with a shoulder roast from smaller animals. For wild game the foil oven bag works very well because there are no vents, but if you use a plastic oven bag just don't poke all those holes in it. One is sufficient. All the moisture you add needs to stay in the bag.

## Ingredients
1/2 pound side pork, chopped (about 1 cup)
2 large yellow onions, sliced
10 cloves garlic, chopped
2 tablespoons sugar
1/4 cup tomato paste
4 cups beef bouillon
1 large foil oven bag
2 pound brisket

## Cooking
1. Preheat the oven to 300°F. In a large skillet, over medium heat gently sauté the chopped side pork. After 4 or 5 minutes, add the onion, garlic, and sugar and continue sautéing until the onions are soft, about 10 minutes.
2. Add the tomato paste and the bouillon to the skillet, and stir it into the onions. Arrange the foil oven bag in a roasting pan, with the opening tipped up. Pour the onions and bouillon mixture into the oven bag, leaving a tablespoon or two of the rendered pork fat in the pan.
3. Lightly brown the brisket on both sides in the remaining fat, then add it to the oven bag. Seal the bag, and gently rotate to make sure it's sealed and to cover the brisket completely with the cooking juices.
4. Bake in the oven until the brisket is tender, about 3 hours. Slice thin, arrange on a platter with egg noodles, and spoon the sauce on top.

## Wild Sides: Sweet and Sour Refrigerator Pickles
Makes 2 quarts

Make these easy pickles 3-5 days ahead to give the vinegar a chance to work on the cukes. Once you know the routine you can vary it, with 1 tablespoon whole mustard seed or a sliced serrano chili to each quart jar.

### Ingredients
2 cups apple cider vinegar
2 cups sugar
3 large cucumbers (about 3 pounds)

### Preparation
1. Get three quart jars clean and ready to use. In the first jar measure out the sugar and vinegar, and cover the jar tightly. Shake the jar, then let it sit on the counter. Repeat until the sugar has dissolved, about ten minutes and three shakes.
2. In the meantime, slice the cucumbers and stuff them into the other two jars. When the sugar has dissolved totally, pour it over the sliced cucumbers. Close both jars tightly and chill at least 48 hours before serving.

*Slice Of The Wild*

# The Tougher End
## Slow Cooking

# Laurel and Chuck's Chuck Roast Sandwich Meat
Makes 8-10 sandwiches

What could be more appropriate than packing a deer sandwich on a deer hunt? Or, in her case, Laurel's last elk on this year's elk hunt. Since chuck roasts (just another name for shoulder roasts) are tougher than rump roasts, this cut is a good fit. But you could use a rump roast if you want, even if it's pretty tender. It just won't take as long to get done.

## Ingredients
2 pound shoulder roast
2 tablespoons oil
1/2 envelope Lipton Onion Soup mix
1 cup hot water

## Cooking
1. Brown the roast over medium-high heat in the oil. When browned on all sides, transfer the roast to the slow cooker.
2. Mix the soup mix with the water and deglaze the pan with this mixture, being sure to scrape up all the caramelized meat bits from the skillet. Pour this over the roast in the slow cooker.
3. Cook on high for one hour, then reduce the heat to low and cook another 6-7 hours until tender. (To use for sandwiches, the roast just has to be tender enough to chew. For the Tex-Mex Pulled Venison recipe in a couple of pages, tender means falling apart--and more cooking time. But you can cook this one until it falls apart if you want.)
4. Remove the roast from the slow cooker, chill, and slice for sandwiches. Moisten with a blend of equal parts mayonnaise and ketchup--or mayo and salsa--or just moisten with prepared Thousand Island dressing.

****Alternately, transfer the roast to a warm platter, and cover with foil to keep warm. Then pour the cooking juices into a saucepan over medium heat. Mix 1/2 cup cream and 1/4 cup flour enough to get the lumps out, and then slowly dribble this mixture into the hot pan juices, stirring continuously until slightly thickened. Slice the roast, pour the gravy over the slices, and serve with mashed potatoes.

## Tips & Tactics: Slow Cooking The Safe Way

We've all done it: started the slow cooker on low and cooked a one-pot-meal all day long at that temperature. According to the newest food science research, we've been lucky not to get sick. The problem is that the low setting takes so long to come up to safe cooking temperatures, that germs can multiply easily.

So convert all your favorite slow cooker recipes: start them with one hour on high, and when everything comes to a low boil, lower the heat to low for the rest of the cooking time.

To give the pot a head start, pour all your liquids into the slow cooker on high, before you even start browning the meat. (And for a nuclear boost, you can microwave some liquids like the bouillon and tomato sauce until not quite boiling before putting them in the slow cooker. Just add them slowly so you don't crack the crockery.)

# Even Better Sandwich Roast

Serves 6-8

Chuck and Laurel's slow cooker recipe will make great sandwich meat, but the problem with lean meat and slow cooking is that it can make the meat dry. Adding a little fat in the cooking sauce, like the mayonnaise in this recipe, may not make the prettiest looking sauce, but it definitely ups the ante on moist meat. Serve this recipe hot or chilled. And don't waste the mayo/tomato sauce. Hot, it livens up the plainest pasta; chilled, it makes a great sandwich spread.)

## Ingredients
- 2-4 pound roast
- 1 teaspoon salt
- 1 teaspoon pepper
- 2 tablespoons oil
- 14.5 ounce can chopped tomatoes
- 1/2 cup mayonnaise

## Cooking

1. Sprinkle the salt and pepper over the roast, and brown on all sides in the oil over medium heat. In the meantime, add the tomatoes (with their juices) and mayonnaise to the slow cooker. Turn the slow cooker onto high heat; stir the mayonnaise into the tomato, and cover. (The cooking sauce should cover at least 3/4 of the roast. If not, double the sauce ingredients.)

2. Transfer the meat to the slow cooker, and cook on high for one hour, then reduce the heat to low and cook another 6-7 hours, turning the roast 2 or 3 times during cooking. Slice and serve on pasta or rice, with green beans on the side. Or transfer to a storage container, with the sauce, and chill. Slice and serve on hard rolls, with the chilled sauce.

## Tips & Tactics: Better Browning for Better Flavor

One of the tricks to a rich-tasting sauce in your stews and roasts is to dry the meat before you brown it. Put drippy meat in hot oil and pretty soon clouds of unappetizing gray liquid billow up. Instead of 'browning' the meat and creating sweet, caramelized meat bits that will enrich your pan juices, you're steaming it—and diluting the flavor in the process. We can fix that.

First, place the meat on a double layer of paper towels, then press another double layer on the top of the meat, and let it sit for 5-10 minutes while you preheat your skillet or oven. That will absorb 90% of the liquid. For smaller pieces—like bite-sized chunks for stews and soups—cut and trim first, then dry.

Second, get the oil in the browning pan sizzling hot before adding the meat. If the first chunk of meat doesn't sizzle when it hits the oil wait for it to sizzle before you add any more. The best thing is to not start browning until you see wisps of smoke start to come off the surface of the pan. Add the meat immediately, and don't worry. The room temperature meat will cool the pan quickly—before the oil burns.

Finally, don't overload the pan. Choose a skillet or Dutch oven that has enough surface area to fit the meat in a single layer with some space between each piece, or just brown in batches, adding and heating a little more oil before starting the second and third batch. (The oil heats very quickly the second time.) If you still end up with clouds of steamy gray liquid, corral the meat with a slotted spoon, and pour off—or spoon up—the steamy goop, very, very carefully. I've been known to throw all caution to the wind and blot it up with paper towels, but as they say on TV, don't try this at home.

Add the drying to your preparation routine, and you'll see a big improvement in flavor. Of course my friend Bob Whitehead, points out that browning the meat at all just dirties a second pan. But we think all that delicious caramelized flavor is worth it.

Slice Of The Wild

# Easy Tex-Mex Pulled Venison
Serves 6-8

The unique flavor in this dish comes from nopalitos: pickled cactus leaves. Of course, the serrano peppers they're pickled with add to the thrill. Yes, the meat takes a long time to cook, but with two of the three major flavors coming pre-packaged, there's not a lot of actual prep time. For moderately to very tough roasts, let this cook overnight for truly pull-apart meat. And if you're pressed, serve the meat without the tortillas. Just don't forget the sour cream.. (As usual, I used mild taco seasoning; use hot if you use tabasco sauce like ketchup.)

## Ingredients
For the slow cooker:
2 cups prepared Bloody Mary mix (no alcohol needed)
1 cup beef bouillon
2 cups water
2 pound neck roast (or other tough roast)
2 tablespoons oil

## To Finish:
2 red onions, sliced
2 red sweet bell peppers, sliced
1/4 cup oil
2 tablespoons Mexican seasoning mix
1 to 2 cups drained nopalitos
6-8 corn tortillas
Sour cream

## Cooking
1. Start a 3 to 5 quart slow cooker on high, and add the Bloody Mary mix, bouillon, and water. Cover the crock. Meanwhile, brown the roast on all sides in 2 tablespoons of oil over medium heat, and transfer to the slow cooker.
2. Cook for 1 hour on high, then turn the slow cooker down to low. Cook until pull-apart tender, 6-12 hours.

## To Finish
1. Once tender, pull the meat apart, saving the cooking liquid. Set the meat aside. In a large skillet, sauté the onion and peppers in the oil over medium heat. Add the seasoning mix and continue cooking until the onions are tender. Add the pulled meat and enough slow cooker liquid to keep the meat looking very moist. (You may end up using more than half of the liquid.) Continue cooking until the meat is hot again, and then gently toss the nopalitos into the mix. Cook another 1 to 2 minutes until the nopalitos are hot.
2. Arrange the meat mixture on the tortillas as you would for tacos, add a dollop of sour cream and enjoy. Or make the Tex-Mex version of a grilled cheese sandwich: a pile of pulled meat, salsa, and sour cream between two tortillas, fried golden brown.

# Cream of Mushroom Slow Cooker Pot Roast
Serves 6-8

This is another of the moister-than-usual dishes, since the mushroom soup adds fat--and moisture--to our naturally lean venison. Make it with the potatoes and carrots as shown, or slice and serve it over Texas toast with lots of gravy.

## Ingredients
1 teaspoon salt
1 teaspoon pepper
2-4 pound roast
2 tablespoons oil
1 can cream of mushroom soup
1 1/3 cups beef bouillon
1 pound red or new potatoes
1 pound carrots

## Cooking
1. Sprinkle the salt and pepper on the roast, and brown on all sides in the oil over medium heat. In the meantime, add the can of soup and beef bouillon to the slow cooker.
2. Turn the slow cooker onto high heat; stir the soup mix and bouillon to blend them, and cover the cooker. (The liquids should cover at least 3/4 of the roast. If not, double the liquids or cut the roast in half to sit lower in the pot.)
3. Transfer the meat to the slow cooker, and continue cooking about 1 hour on high; then turn to low and cook another 6-7 hours, turning the roast 2 or 3 times during cooking.
4. Midway through the cooking add quartered potatoes and carrots. (Allow at least 2 hours on low.) Serve hot as a one-dish meal, or omit the vegetables and serve hot over toast with plenty of gravy.

## Tips & Tactics: Why Slow Cook?
There are lots of reasons slow cookers are one of the cook's best friends. Let's start with the fact that unlike ovens, they don't heat up the kitchen, so you can have a hot meal on hot, muggy, summer days. (Or cook, and then chill the meat for the best of hot, muggy day meals.)

But let's not forget the real purpose of a slow cooker: to cook slowly and with moisture. If you have any doubts regarding the chewiness of your venison, or simply insist on all meat being cooked well-done, slow and moist is the safest way to get tender results.

So what works as a side dish with these slow cooked roasts? To serve this Cream of Mushroom Pot Roast hot, a side of Half Mashed Potatoes or Super Creamy Mac & Cheese are easy and filling; served cold, the Old World Ale Roast works well with Traditional Potato Salad; and the Tex-Mex Potato Salad is a welcome change, at least now and then, from tortillas when munching on a chilled Tex-Mex Pulled Venison roast.

# Alfredo Pot Roast and Sandwich Meat
Serves 6-8

I don't know how much easier dinner can get--or how tasty. This is a stick-to-your-ribs, cold-weather, comfort-food dish that doesn't require a vast array of ingredients or culinary skill. I prefer egg noodles with this easy Alfredo, but the sauce is so rich that mashed potatoes or rice are just as satisfying.

## Ingredients
1 teaspoon salt
1 teaspoon pepper
2-4 pound roast
2 tablespoons oil
15 ounce bottle Bertolli's Alfredo sauce
1 cup beef bouillon

## Cooking
1. Sprinkle the salt and pepper on the roast, and brown on all sides in the oil over medium heat. In the meantime, add the Alfredo sauce and beef bouillon to the slow cooker.
2. Turn the slow cooker onto high heat; stir the soup mix and bouillon to blend them, and cover. (The liquids should cover at least 3/4 of the roast. If not, double the liquids or cut the roast in half to sit lower in the pot.)
3. Transfer the meat to the slow cooker, and cook on high another hour, then reduce the heat to low and cook another 6-7 hours, turning the roast 2 or 3 times during cooking.
4. Midway through the cooking add quartered potatoes and carrots. (Allow at least 2 hours on low.) Serve hot with egg noodles and salad on the side. (You can re-use the sauce for another pot roast, if you do the sandwich option.)

Slice Of The Wild

# Old World Slow Cooker Ale Roast
Serves 6-8

The bacon in this slow cooker roast makes for a rich, complex and tasty roast. Serve it over egg noodles or as a hot French Dip-type sandwich. All you'd need for the sandwich is a hard roll; you'll have lots of au jus in the cooker.

## Ingredients
1 teaspoon salt
1 teaspoon pepper
2-4 pound roast
2 slices bacon
12 ounce bottle Pale Ale (or lager beer)
6 tablespoons red currant jelly
1 cup beef bouillon
3 whole bay leaves
1 tablespoon minced fresh thyme

## Cooking
1. Rub the salt and pepper on all sides of the roast. Lightly brown the bacon over medium heat, then transfer the bacon to the slow cooker. Brown the roast in the bacon fat on all sides.
2. In the meantime, turn the slow cooker onto high heat; add the rest of the ingredients and give them a stir. (The cooking sauce should cover at least 3/4 of the roast. If not, double the sauce ingredients or cut the roast to sit lower in the pot.)
3. Transfer the meat to the slow cooker, and cook on high for one hour. Reduce the heat to low and cook another 6-7 hours, turning the roast 2 or 3 times during cooking.
4. Serve hot, with lots of the sauce over rice. Or slice hot, and serve on hard rolls as a French Dip sandwich with a side of Traditional Potato Salad.

## Wild Sides: Traditional Potato Salad
Serves 6-8

Sometimes the same old same old is just right. In this case it's potato salad like my grandmother used to make—but with modern lower fat sensibilities taken into account.

## Ingredients
1 1/2 pounds potatoes
1/2 yellow onion, chopped
2 eggs
1/2 cup mayonnaise
1/4 cup apple cider vinegar
1/2 teaspoon celery salt
2 teaspoons sugar
1/2 teaspoon salt
1 teaspoon coarse black pepper

## Preparation
1. Boil the potatoes until just fork-tender. (About 20 minutes for medium sized potatoes; more for bigger ones.) Boil the eggs. Cool both with running cold water, then chill 1-2 hours.
2. Chop the chilled potatoes and eggs into a large bowl with the onion. In a small bowl, mix the rest of the ingredients. Gently toss the mayonnaise mixture into the potatoes. Cover, chill, and then serve.

**Perfect Boiled Eggs**: Poke a hole in the fat end of each egg with a safety pin, then place in a saucepan just large enough to hold a single layer. Cover with cold water. Bring to a boil; reduce the heat to low; simmer 2 minutes. Turn the heat off, cover the pot, and let the eggs sit another 15 minutes. Pour cold water over the eggs, chill, then peel and chop.

# Fall-Apart Oven Pot Roast
Serves 6-8

The difference between a tender pot roast that will slice up easily for sandwiches and a pot roast that falls apart when you try to lift it from the pot is simply a matter of time. And while you'll never run out of liquid in a slow cooker, this oven method takes 1/4 the time and concentrates the sauce to a delicious degree. This is a great come-home-from-hunting one-dish meal on a cold November day, but John is just as likely to pile these falling-apart chunks between two slices of toast. (If you can't find winter savory, use marjoram.)

## Ingredients
3 slices side pork, chopped (about 1 cup)
2 to 3 pound shoulder roast
1 cup Madeira
1 pound bag frozen pearl onions, thawed
1 pound bag baby carrots
2 cups beef bouillon
1 tablespoon dried leaf winter savory
1 teaspoon coarse black pepper

## Cooking
1. Preheat the oven to 325°F. In a 3-quart Dutch oven over medium heat, brown the side pork until it releases about 2 tablespoons of grease; then brown the shoulder roast in the side pork and its fat.
2. Leaving the meat in the pot, deglaze the pan with the Madeira. (Pour it into a measuring cup first.) Continue cooking until the Madeira is reduced to about 1/3 the volume, 5-6 minutes.
3. Add the rest of the ingredients, cover the pot and transfer to the oven. Cook 2 1/2 to 3 hours or until the meat falls apart when you try to lift it out of the pot. (If you tied the roast during butchering, untie it before cooking. And check the liquid once during cooking. There should be sauce at the table.) Break the pot-roasted meat into chunks with a spoon.
4. Serve over pasta or rice, or heat a loaf of Pepperidge Farm garlic bread, divide into 3 or 4 individual servings, and serve it over that.

# Wild Sides: Scalloped Pineapple
Serves 8

I have been cooking this recipe—and sharing it with readers—since I first tasted this dish at White Oak Plantation in Alabama more than a decade ago. They wish I'd stop, because their hunters have come to expect it. And once you try it, you'll know why. And, yes, technically it's a dessert, but when I had it at White Oak the first time, it was served with the vegetables. Who am I to dispute that? After all, they know turkey and whitetail hunting like nobody's business.

## Ingredients
2 cups sugar
1/4 cup margarine
4 eggs
1/4 cup milk
20 ounce can crushed pineapple
4 cups cubed white bread, crusts removed

## Cooking
1. Preheat the oven to 375°F. In a large bowl, cream the sugar, margarine and eggs together until very smooth.
2. Stir the milk and pineapple into the egg mixture. Gently toss the bread cubes into this mixture.
3. Pour the batter into a 9-inch square baking dish and bake 15 minutes at 375°F; reduce the heat to 350°F and bake one hour more. Serve hot with ice cream or whipped cream. (It's also good cold, with coffee.)

# Pot Roast with Sour Cream Gravy
Serves 8-10

Don't get intimidated by the serving size. We often make a roast this size just for the two of us on Saturday morning, then graze on it all weekend, (reheating gently in the microwave). Pot roast is the classic slow, moist cooking method for tougher cuts. If we were cooking beef, it would be a chuck roast--the meat around the shoulder blade--but use any venison roast that you suspect will be too tough for dry-roasting. And please notice how quick gravy is to make with a little bit of sour cream. It's a stirring moment--literally.

## Ingredients
5 to 6 pound roast
1 teaspoon salt
1 teaspoon pepper
2 tablespoons oil
2 pounds carrots, whole
1 pound onions, quartered
2 pounds potatoes, quartered
1 can or bottle beer, 12 ounces
2 teaspoons dried leaf thyme
2 tablespoons flour
1/2 cup cold water
1/3 cup sour cream

## Cooking
1. Preheat the oven to 325°F. Pat the roast dry with paper towels and season with salt and pepper. In a large skillet on medium-high heat, heat the oil and brown all sides and ends of the roast.
2. Transfer the roast to a large, covered roasting pan. Arrange the carrots, onions, and potatoes around the roast, pour the beer over the top, sprinkle with the thyme, and cover. Roast 3 to 4 hours, until the meat falls from the bone. (Check the moisture level after 2 hours, and replenish if necessary.)
3. Remove the roast to a cutting board. Turn the oven off. Transfer the vegetables onto a serving platter, cover and place in the oven. Add beef bouillon to the pan juices, if you don't have at least 3 cups of pan juices for the gravy, and start on medium-high heat.
4. Bring the pan juices to a low boil on the range top. Dissolve the flour into the cold water, add to the pan, then reduce the heat to low, and stir until the gravy has thickened. Stir in the sour cream and simmer for 2 to 3 minutes longer until hot.
5. To serve, cut the roast in thick slices, arrange with the vegetables on the serving platter and pour the gravy over the top. Or do as John and I do: leave everything in the roasting pan and dole out individual servings over the course of the weekend. (If your roaster fits in the fridge; if not, do whatever's easy...)

# Sauer Pot Roast
Serves 6

Here's a good use for a tougher chunk of meat. You get the long marinated effect of a sauerbraten, but only marinate for 48 hours. Take the shoulder meat, a piece of elk or moose brisket, or anything from a tougher animal. Just don't waste a good piece of tenderloin. It won't hold up.

## Ingredients
1 cup beef bouillon
2 tablespoons sweet hot mustard
2 tablespoons red wine vinegar
4 tablespoons brown sugar
2 pound boneless roast
5 slices bacon, cut in chunks
8 potatoes, quartered
6 carrots, sliced in half
1/2 medium large red cabbage, cored and quartered
6 ginger snaps

## Preparation
1. Combine the bouillon, mustard, vinegar, and brown sugar in a non-corrosive bowl or plastic bag. Put the meat in the marinade, and the marinade in the refrigerator for 48 hours, turning every 8 hours.
2. When you're ready to cook, remove the roast from the marinade and dry it with paper towels. Save the marinade.

## Cooking
1. In a 3 to 5-quart Dutch oven, over medium heat, brown the bacon. Remove the bacon, and drain on paper towels. Pour off all but 2 tablespoons of the fat. Brown the roast on all sides in the fat over medium-high heat.
2. Return the bacon to the pan, and add the reserved marinade, potatoes, and carrots. Bring the sauce to a boil, cover, and turn the heat down to a simmer. Simmer for 60 minutes, until the meat is tender, and then add the cabbage. Simmer for 30 minutes more.
3. To serve, transfer the meat and vegetables to a warm platter and cover loosely. Bring the pan juices to a simmer. Crumble the ginger snaps and add them to the pan, stirring constantly until the gravy thickens. Pour the gravy over the meat and vegetables and serve.

****To warm a platter, turn the oven to 200°F; once it reaches that temperature, set the platter in the center of the oven, and turn the oven off. (If the oven is already in use, pour some water on the platter and microwave on high for 30 seconds just before you need it. Dry and use.)

# Slow Cooker Venison Stroganoff
Serves 6-8

Really pressed for time? You could skip browning the meat, but you'll lose a lot of flavor. It's called the Maillard reaction: browning the proteins of meat makes the meat sweeter and richer in flavor. For me, that's as much a palate-pleaser as the fat in the sour cream. As with the other recipes that call for browning the meat first, dry the meat and avoid the evil gray steam.

## Ingredients
1 cup red wine
2 teaspoons beef bouillon granules
3 cups hot water
1 cup sour cream, divided
1 teaspoon dried leaf thyme
1 teaspoon salt
1 teaspoon coarse ground black pepper
10 g. (.35 ounce) bag dried porcini mushrooms, broken up
2 pounds venison steaks, cut in thin strips
1/4 cup butter, divided
1/4 cup oil, divided
1 medium yellow onion, minced very fine (almost pureed)
2 cloves garlic, minced
2 pound bag of egg noodles

## Preparation
1. In a 5-quart slow cooker, start the red wine, beef bouillon granules, water, 1/2 cup of the sour cream, thyme, salt, pepper, and porcini mushrooms on high. Dry the venison strips in paper towels.
1. Over medium-high heat, add 1 tablespoon each of the butter and oil to a medium skillet and heat until the butter begins to brown. (You'll smell it caramelizing; but don't let it go past a sizzling golden brown.) Turn the heat down to medium and start browning the venison strips, in 3 to 4 batches, about 4-5 minutes per batch until the edges get a little dark brown. Add a little more butter and oil for each batch as necessary. Transfer the browned meat to the slow cooker.
2. When all the meat is browned, add the last butter/oil and let it get golden brown again over medium heat; add the minced onion and garlic. Stir into the butter, and sauté until the onions are golden brown, about 5-7 minutes. Add to the slow cooker.
3. Cover the slow cooker, turn it down to medium, and let the Stroganoff cook 6-8 hours.
4. To serve: While you prepare the egg noodles according to package directions, ladle out about 1 cup of the slow cooker sauce and stir the rest of the sour cream (1/2 cup) into it; add that back to the slow cooker, stir well. Serve over egg noodles.

# Hunter's Hot Pot
Serves 6-8

I don't live where people are addicted to eating raw tuna in sea urchin sauce. (Thank goodness.) I live where I can hunt. Every day if I want to. So, when I cook game--and share recipes in my cookbooks--I look for ingredients that can be found in places that don't cater to the sea urchin crowd. And since I don't have any more spare time than you do, I stick to easy, quick to start, cooking methods. This Hot Pot may be the best example of that philosophy. It cooks without supervision, is made from ingredients I can buy at Bob's Thriftway (summer hours 6am to midnight), and tastes better than any instant dinner-in-a-box.

## Ingredients
2 pounds stew meat, cubed and dried
1/4 cup oil
1 medium yellow onion, sliced
1/2 cup Kraft Catalina salad dressing
28-ounce can chopped tomatoes
2 cups hot water
1/2 teaspoon salt
1/2 teaspoon black pepper
1/4 cup raw rice

## Cooking
1. Preheat the oven to 300°F. In a 3-quart Dutch oven, brown the meat in the oil over medium-high heat, about 4-5 minutes a batch. For best results brown in two or three batches starting with part of the oil, adding more, and letting it heat up before you add the meat.
2. Add the onion to the pot with the last batch, and stir it into the meat. Cook 3-5 more minutes, until you start to smell the onions and they begin to take on a light brown color.
3. Pour the Catalina dressing into the pot and stir it into the meat and onions. With a spatula, loosen all those golden caramelized bits of meat from the bottom of the pot and stir them into the sauce.
4. When the sauce comes to a sizzle, return the other browned meat to the pot, and stir it into the sauce. Add the tomatoes, hot water, salt, pepper, and rice and give the pot one more stir.
5. Let the stew come to a low simmer, cover, and transfer the Dutch oven to the center of the preheated oven. Let the stew cook 2 hours, or until the meat is tender. To turn your stew into a pot pie with real class, put a lid on it.

## Wild Sides: Put a Lid on It
Putting the comfort in comfort food is easy with this Hot Pot and a roll of refrigerated bread sticks. You can even make a lattice work crust, like the photo in the center photo section.

Start by taking the cover off the Dutch oven and raising the oven temperature to 400°F. Unroll the bread sticks as per the package directions, but then stretch them out a bit either by pulling gently, or just letting them swing gently between your hands just long enough so that a few will stretch across the Dutch oven. Don't twist them.

Lay the breadsticks across the top of the stew in a grid. Leave the top off, but close the oven door, and bake until the breadsticks are golden brown, about 15 minutes.

Serve hot.

# Rib-Sticking Stew
Serves 6-8

Dredging the meat in flour before browning it not only keeps you from getting splattered when the moist meat meets hot grease, but when you add the bouillon, the stew makes its own, no-lump, gravy.

## Ingredients
1/2 cup flour
2 pounds cubed stew meat
1 tablespoon beef bouillon granules, dissolved in
2 cups hot water
1/4 cup oil
1/2 cup medium dry sherry
3 tablespoons Worcestershire sauce
3 tablespoons red currant jelly
1 bay leaf
1 teaspoon dried leaf thyme
2 teaspoons dried leaf oregano
1 teaspoon salt
1/2 teaspoon pepper
1 medium yellow onion, cut in chunks
6-8 medium carrots, in chunks
6 medium potatoes, quartered

## Cooking
1. Measure the flour into a plastic bag and toss the stew meat inside until all sides are coated. Set aside. Stir the bouillon granules into the water.
2. In a 3 to 4-quart Dutch oven, brown the meat in the oil over medium high heat, about 4-5 minutes per batch. Add the sherry to deglaze the pan after the last batch, stirring up the tasty bits from the bottom of the pan. Return all the meat to the Dutch oven and stir into the sauce.
3. When the sherry has all but evaporated, stir the beef bouillon into the pot, then add the Worcestershire sauce, jelly, bay leaf, thyme, oregano, salt, and pepper. Bring the pot to a slow simmer, add the onion, carrots, and potatoes, give it a stir, and then cover it. Let it simmer on low, 1 to 2 hours, or until tender.

# Too Much To Stew Stew
Serves 6

Got real lucky last fall? Have a nice, tough trophy deer or elk in the freezer? My guess is you're running out of tasty ways to fix him. Then try this one, with a bit of trendy balsamic vinegar, but no trendy cooking methods. This one leans toward 'savory' flavors: manly, meaty, an excellent contrast to the slightly sweet taste of Meredith's Secret Ingredient Stew. Like the Wild Rice and Red Wine Hot Pot, I'm adding salt at the end. This time it's the salt in the balsamic vinegar that's the unknown factor.

## Ingredients
2 pounds stew meat, cut in bite sized chunks
2 tablespoons oil
1/2 cup balsamic vinegar
2 cups beef bouillon
1 pound frozen pearl onions, thawed
2 tablespoons butter
2 teaspoons sugar
1 teaspoon dried leaf thyme
1 teaspoon dried leaf oregano
1 teaspoon coarse ground black pepper
1 pound carrots, chopped
1 rutabaga, chopped
1/2 cup wild rice
4 cups hot water

## Cooking
1. In a 3 to 5-quart Dutch oven, brown the meat in oil, starting on medium-high heat. When you turn the meat, lower the heat to medium. Cook in batches if you need to. Once all the meat is browned, return all to the pan, and add the balsamic vinegar. Bring the sauce to a simmer, and reduce the heat to low as you stir up the tasty bits of caramelized meat from the bottom. Let the vinegar reduce to about 1/4 of its volume (4-5 minutes), then add the bouillon.
2. Drain the liquid off the thawed onions and pat them with a paper towel until fairly dry. In a (separate) large skillet over medium high heat, melt the butter. Add the onions once the butter is sizzling, and when it start sizzling again, reduce the heat to medium. Stir the sugar, thyme, oregano, and black pepper into the onions, and continue cooking until they are golden brown. Stir the onion mixture into the stew.
3. Now add the carrots, rutabaga, rice, and water, and bring to a low boil. Reduce the heat to a simmer, and cook 90 minutes, or until the rice and meat are tender.
4. Ladle into bowls and sprinkle a bit of kosher salt to taste on each serving. Depending on the bouillon and vinegar you use, the salt can vary, so it's a good idea to not add any until the end, when you know what you have.

Slice Of The Wild

# Boone's Stew
Serves 6

I'm not sure you can have too many recipes for things that cook by themselves and are ready and waiting whenever you, or guests, show up to eat. Of course the cooking time will depend on how tough the cut and animal is. For moderate to pretty tough meat, 45 to 90 minutes is usually sufficient. So gauge your cut and always err on the side of too much cooking. This is another of those times when more is better.

## Ingredients
2 pounds stew meat in 1-inch chunks
1 large onion, sliced
3 tablespoons oil
1/3 cup barley
1/3 cup wild rice
2 cups beef bouillon
1 cup water
15 ounce can chopped tomatoes
1 tablespoon Worcestershire sauce
2 cloves garlic, minced
1 teaspoon Montreal Steak Seasoning

## Cooking
1. Brown the meat and onions in the oil over medium heat in a 3 to 5-quart Dutch oven.
2. Add the rest of the ingredients and bring the mixture to a low boil. Turn the heat down to a simmer, cover, and let simmer very slowly 45 minutes, or until the meat is tender. For a simple pot pie conversion, look to your right.

## Wild Sides: Individual Pot Pies
You can make one big pot pie as in the Hunter's Hot Pot, but I prefer an having my own private pot pie with an artsy crescent roll on top. (That way, hopefully, no one hogs the crust.) It's even easier than the all in one pot pie.

Instead of using refrigerator bread sticks, open a package of refrigerator crescent rolls, and roll them out on the counter. Slice each in half.

Preheat the oven to 375°F. Pour out the soup in to individual bowls and set the bowls on a cookie sheet in the center of the oven.

Lay a half roll flat across each serving, and bake 15 minutes or until a good warm brown. (The underside tends to be undercooked if you don't brown the top enough.)

Serve hot.

tougher ◇ stew meat ◇ cover & cook

Slice Of The Wild

# Meredith's Secret Ingredient Stew
Serves 8

Meredith Stephens ran the best small town bar I ever saw. She was what my grandmother would have called a pistol: bootlegging movies off her satellite dish and renting them for a buck a day; duct-taping a Daily Trivia Question on the back bar mirror, and keeping a 'Don't Say *%$' Jar on the bar (everyone said it, including Meredith, but quarters collected paid for a party she threw for the town every 4th of July); or creating recipes with secret ingredients that have lived on long after her. Use a larger slow cooker for this one: at least 4 quart capacity. (This was the only secret she ever revealed and I still wonder if she told all.)

## Ingredients
2 cups beef bouillon
2 cups hot water
20 ounce can pineapple chunks, drained and juice saved
1/2 cup flour
1 teaspoon garlic salt
1 teaspoon white pepper
1/4 teaspoon cayenne pepper
1 1/2 pounds venison stew meat, cubed
1/4 cup plus 2 tablespoons oil, in all
1 teaspoon smoked Chipotle Tabasco sauce
1 large yellow onion, sliced
1 teaspoon sugar
1 pound potatoes, diced
1 pound carrots, sliced

## Cooking
1. Start the slow cooker on high, and add the beef bouillon, water, and the pineapple chunks. (Save the pineapple juice you drained off for deglazing the pan.) In a plastic bag combine the flour, garlic salt, white and cayenne peppers, and shake. Add the venison cubes, seal the bag and shake until the meat is lightly covered.
3. Brown the meat in the oil over medium heat until golden, then add the pineapple juice and Tabasco sauce slowly into the browning meat. Scrape up the tasty bits from the bottom of the pan, and when the sauce thickens, pour the meat and sauce into the slow cooker.
4. Add 2 tablespoons more oil and the sugar to the pan and start browning the onions on medium-high heat. Once they sizzle, lower the heat to medium. Continue browning the onions until they smell very sweet, about 15 minutes. Add them to the slow cooker, too.
5. Add the potatoes and carrots, stir them into the stew, and cover. When the pot comes to a slow simmer, reduce the heat to low. Continue cooking 8 hours. Serve hot with lots of attitude.

# All Day Beer Stew

Serves 6-8

Since we're a 2-person household, I like to cook a smaller stew sometimes. Since a slow cooker is very gentle, even a half-full stew won't burn, and the vinegar speeds up the effect of moist heat on tough meat. You can use any lager beer for this from the cheapest convenience store beer to a better micro-brew. Or for a change of pace, some ales give the dish a deeper but tarter flavor.

## Ingredients

12 ounce can of beer
1 cup beef bouillon
2 pounds tougher steak, cubed
3 tablespoons oil, in all
1 large yellow onion, sliced
1 gala (or other sweet apple), chopped
1/2 cup apple cider vinegar
2 pounds red potatoes, chopped
2 cups red cabbage, chopped
2 teaspoons dried leaf thyme
1 teaspoon bacon bits
1 teaspoon coarse ground black pepper
1 teaspoon salt

## Cooking

1. Start the slow cooker on high. Pour in the beer and bouillon.
2. In a large skillet, brown the steak chunks on all sides in 2 tablespoons of the oil starting on high heat. When you turn the meat, reduce the heat to medium. Transfer the meat to the slow cooker as it browns.
3. Add the third tablespoon of oil, and brown the onions and apple chunks until soft, about 5-7 minutes. Add them to the pot, too. Deglaze the pan with the apple cider vinegar, letting it simmer enough to reduce to about 1/4 cup. Scrape that and the pan drippings into the pot.
4. Add the rest of the ingredients to the slow cooker, reduce the heat to low, cover and cook 8 hours. As with all stews, soups and pot roasts, if you can let it go a second day, it will be even better.

## Tips & Tactics: Deglazing the Pan

Deglazing a pan saves the flavor you created when browning the meat, enhances the flavor of the sauce you'll eventually serve at the table, and makes you look like a pro.

Some would have us believe that deglazing began with the legions of slaves who worked in the kitchens of pre-guillotine French kings and noblemen, the source of all that hi-blown gourmet cuisine lifestyle magazines try to guilt trip us into. But, at it's most basic level, deglazing a pan is no more chic than sopping up excess gravy with a wadded up chunk of Wonder® Bread, except you do it with a liquid.

And, yes, we've been doing it all along--whenever we added liquid to browned meat while the pan was hot, and didn't toss that liquid away, we deglazed. French nobility could just afford a higher grade of Wonder Bread.

There's a lot of deglazing going on in this cookbook. Apple cider vinegar here, Madeira there. And while the cheapest Madeira is a tasty deglazer, as always the better the quality of the ingredients, the better the finished product. You will get fine results using what's easily available, but if you have the access and budget to buy better Wonder Bread, go for it.

# Wild Rice and Red Wine Hot Pot
Serves 6

You'll notice the salt in this dish is only added at the end. That's because when you deglaze the pan with red wine it concentrates the wine--as well as the salt in the wine. How much? It depends on the red wine--they vary in salt content--and how concentrated it gets. That's why I add the salt at the table. And since I'm adding it at the table, I use kosher salt because I can use less and still get that salt zing. (Yes, Bob's Thriftway sells Morton's Kosher Salt, in an inexpensive 3-pound box. The exotic mushroom medley I buy in Helena.)

## Ingredients

- 1 1/2 cups dry red wine (like Merlot)
- 1/4 ounce bag dried exotic mushroom medley
- 1 cup beef bouillon
- 3 cups water
- 1 pound bag frozen pearl onions, thawed
- 3 pounds tough venison steaks, 3/4" cubes
- 3 tablespoons oil, in all
- 1 red bell pepper, chopped
- 1 tablespoon minced garlic
- 1 pound carrots, diced
- 1/2 cup (uncooked) wild rice
- 1 whole clove
- 1/4 teaspoon coarse black pepper
- 1/4 cup red currant jelly
- Sour cream
- Kosher salt

## Preparation

In a small bowl, pour the red wine over the dried mushrooms and let them soak 2-3 hours. If you're pressed for time, powder the dried mushrooms in a food processor and add to the wine. Use immediately.

## Cooking

1. Start the slow cooker on high, and stir the beef bouillon, water, and pearl onions into it.
2. In a large skillet, brown the venison chunks in oil, starting at high heat. When you turn the meat, lower the heat to medium. Cook in batches, and transfer the meat to the slow cooker as it gets browned. Add the last tablespoon of oil and sauté the sweet red pepper and garlic until soft and golden. Add to the slow cooker.
3. Deglaze the pan with the red wine and soaked mushrooms, and let that simmer about 3-4 minutes until thoroughly heated. Add the carrots, rice, clove, pepper, and jelly, cover the cooker and let cook 8 hours.
4. To serve, give each helping 1 tablespoon of sour cream and a pinch or two of kosher salt, to taste.

# Tough & Tougher Burger

# Wild-Tamer Hamburgers
Serves 4

When you grind your own venison, you can add fat or not. For these burgers, we don't add fat; they have enough fat in the sour cream and egg that the burgers hold together well. Plus, the extra liquid from the puréed onion makes these venison burgers moist and tasty. But if you have already added the fat, no problem. You'll have a little more fat rendered in the pan, but the taste and texture will still delight.

## Ingredients
1 pound ground venison
2 tablespoons puréed onion
2 tablespoons sour cream
1/4 teaspoon garlic powder
1 teaspoon salt
1/2 teaspoon coarse ground black pepper
1 large egg, beaten
2 tablespoons oil

## Preparation
Combine the ground venison, puréed onion, sour cream, garlic powder, salt, pepper, and beaten egg, and refrigerate, covered, 4-24 hours. Shape into four burgers.

## Cooking
1. In a skillet: heat the oil over medium-high heat. When the oil sizzles, place burgers in the skillet. When the meat starts to sizzle, turn the heat down to medium and cook about 3-4 minutes per side, until all the pink is gone in the middle. To finish the insides: cover the skillet, and turn the heat down to low. Cook about 4 minutes more or until there's no pink inside.
2. On the grill: preheat the grill to medium-high heat; wipe a bit of oil on the burgers to prevent sticking. Place them on the cooking rack. Turn only once, after the bottom has cooked 3-4 minutes and is firm enough to hold together when you turn them. Cook until all the pink is gone from the middle, about 8-10 minutes, total.

****For those who like more heat, add 1/2 to 1 teaspoon of red pepper flakes to the mix; and for those watching their fat intake, and simply can't eat both egg AND sour cream in one dish, substitute no-fat sour cream. You won't get quite the rich sour cream flavor, but you'll still have the moisture.

## Tips & Tactics: Avoiding the Dreaded Crumbleburger

There are two not-so-secret secrets to keeping burgers from falling apart on the grill and in the skillet. The first is to add fat. A lot of people add 10 to 30% beef suet to ground venison. Others add oil--even olive oil--when shaping the patties. (Use 1-2 tablespoon of oil per pound of burger.)

The second trick is to let the first side cook long enough that it forms a bit of a hardened crust, about 4-5 minutes depending on the heat. If you wait until that underside is getting nicely browned, it's as if the meat molecules are linking arms. Your ground meat will stay together better even if no fat was added while grinding.

The simplest thing, however, is to be gentle--and only flip once. Your burger has already been through the mill, so flip with kindness.

# Garden Burgers

Serves 4

For me, the best time for garden burgers is when I have lots of herbs growing in and around my tomato plants in the garden. But in many places fresh herbs are a year-round thing in the grocery store. Either way, it's a great way to enjoy a different flavor in America's favorite sandwich.

## Ingredients
1 pound ground venison
2 tablespoons olive oil
2 cloves garlic minced
4 green onions, chopped (include both green and white part)
2 tablespoons fresh sweet basil, minced
1 teaspoon salt
1/2 teaspoon pepper

## Preparation
Combine all the ingredients and refrigerate, covered, 4-24 hours. Shape into four burgers.

## Cooking
1. In a skillet: heat 1 tablespoon oil over medium high heat, until the oil sizzles. Place burgers in skillet. When the meat gets sizzling, turn the heat down to medium and cook about 3-4 minutes per side, until all the pink is gone in the middle. Alternately, after you've seared both sides, cover the skillet, and turn the heat down to low. Cook about 4 minutes more or until there's no pink inside.
2. On the grill: preheat the grill to medium-high heat; wipe a bit of oil on the burgers to prevent sticking. Place them on the cooking rack. Turn only once, after the bottom has cooked 3-4 minutes and is firm enough to turn. (That, and a little added fat are the secrets to keeping venison burgers from falling apart on the grill.) Cook until all the pink is gone from the middle, about 8-10 minutes, total.

# Wild Sides: Mexican Rice

This is a moderately spicy dish. John likes his as is; I add a little sour cream at the table to mellow it out. But we both agree Mexican Rice is a winter staple at our house.

## Ingredients
1 yellow onion, sliced thin
2 tablespoons oil
2 tablespoons butter
2 cups rice, raw
14 ounce can red enchilada sauce (mild)
2 cups beef bouillon
1 cup water

## Cooking
1. Sauté the onion in the oil and butter over medium heat until golden brown. Stir the rice into the onions and sauté together about 1 minute, until the rice starts to brown, then add the enchilada sauce, bouillon and water.
2. Bring the liquids to a low simmer, cover, and reduce the heat to low. Cook about 40 minutes, or until all the liquid is absorbed.

# Burgers with Super Catsup
Serves 4

Who says venison is dry? Buy yourself some good hard rolls at the bakery, split them, and slather a bit of butter on before toasting them on the grill. Then make these burgers and add the Super Catsup.

## Ingredients
1/2 cup bottled sun dried tomato spread
1/2 cup mayonnaise
1 1/2 pound ground venison
2 tablespoons oil
1 teaspoon salt
1/2 teaspoon black pepper
4 hard rolls

## Cooking
1. For the super catsup: combine the sun-dried tomato spread and mayo in a small bowl, mix, cover and refrigerate.
2. In a large bowl, mix the ground venison, oil, salt, and pepper. Set aside, and preheat the grill to medium-high.
3. Lightly oil the burgers and place on the grill. Do not turn until blood begins to appear on the top of the burger and the edges of the bottom--or cooking surface--look well browned. (This, and the oil, keeps the burgers from falling apart on the grill.)
4. When you do turn the burgers, gently, split and butter the inside of the hard rolls. (If you want to spice it up, use one of the herbed butters at the start of the steak section. Place the split rolls butter-side down on the grill while the burgers finish cooking.
5. Cook the burgers about as long on the second side as the first, until there is no pink inside, about 10 minutes for 1-inch thick patties. Place each patty on a bun, and slather with Super Catsup.

# Wild Sides: Country-Style Potato Salad
Serves 6

## Ingredients
1 pound red potatoes
2 eggs
1/2 yellow onion, chopped
1/4 cup mayonnaise
1 tablespoon apple cider vinegar
1 tablespoon country-style Dijon mustard
1 teaspoon sugar
1 teaspoon salt

## Preparation
1. Boil the potatoes until just fork-tender. (About 20 minutes for medium sized potatoes; more for bigger ones.) Boil the eggs. Cool both under cold running water, then transfer to a plate and refrigerate 1-2 hours.
2. Chop the chilled potatoes and eggs into a large bowl with the onion. In a small bowl, combine the mayonnaise, apple cider vinegar, mustard, sugar, and salt. Gently toss the mayonnaise mixture into the potatoes.
3. Cover, chill, and then serve.

# Spiced Burger Skewers
Makes 8 skewers

A little care please in molding these kabobs; it's just ground meat after all. Venison burger with beef suet added will hold together better than straight venison. (Add the egg either way, but for un-fatted venison the egg is vital.) But once cooked, these kabobs will light up your dinner menu.

## Ingredients
1 pound ground venison
1 egg, beaten
1 teaspoon garlic salt
1/2 teaspoon ground coriander
1/2 cup mayonnaise
1/2 cup Heinz chili sauce
1/2 teaspoon Chipotle Tabasco pepper sauce
8 wooden skewers

## Preparation
1. Mix the venison, egg, garlic salt, and coriander thoroughly, and cover. In a separate bowl, combine the mayonnaise, chili sauce, and chipotle Tabasco, and cover. Refrigerate both overnight.
2. Thirty minutes before starting the grill, cover the wooden skewers with cold water, and let them soak.

## Cooking
1. Preheat the grill to 350° to 400°F. Divide the meat mixture into 8 equal parts and shape onto the skewers, gently, molding it into a 1-inch thick, 4-5" long kabob, and place on a lightly oiled length of foil.
2. Slide the foil onto a plate or cutting board to transfer it to the grill. Cook 7 minutes on the first side, gently turn (tongs make it easier), and cook about 5 more minutes on the second side. (Leave them on the foil for easier handling.)
3. Serve dipped in the mayo/chili sauce mixture with a side of Roundup Salad.

# Wild Sides: Roundup Salad
Serves 8

This recipe has morphed over the years from it's exotic middle eastern roots to a great dog day, pot luck bring-along. I guess Roundup is Montanan for tabouli. Freely translated, tabouli is definitely Middle Eastern for no cooking required.

## Ingredients
1 cup cracked wheat (bulgar)
1 1/2 cups cold water
Juice of one lemon
3 cloves garlic
1/4 cup olive oil
1 cup chopped red onion
2 ripe Roma tomatoes, diced
1 cup diced cucumber
5 green onions, diced
1/2 cup chopped red sweet bell pepper
1/2 up minced cilantro
1 teaspoon salt
1 teaspoon coarse black pepper

## Preparation
1. Pour the bulgar into a medium-sized bowl, and add the water. Let it soak 30 minutes.
2. In a blender, puree the lemon juice, garlic cloves, olive oil and red onion.
3. In a large bowl, combine the pureed mixture with the diced tomato, cucumber, green onion, red bell pepper, cilantro, salt, and pepper. When the bulgar has absorbed all the water, toss it gently into the vegetables. Chill before serving.

# Date-Night Burgers with Mushroom Sauce
Serves 4

Forget the special sauce, lettuce, cheese, pickles, onions, and the sesame seed bun. These burgers will set the mood a lot better than a bit of yellow plastic. Oh, and use the mushrooms of your choice. Simple white ones work, but earthier portobello mushrooms are even better. Just be sure to use fresh ones, and real butter.

## Ingredients
1 pound ground venison
3 tablespoons oil, in all
1 egg, beaten
12 ounces fresh mushrooms
1/4 cup butter
1/4 cup beef bouillon
1/4 teaspoon coarse black pepper
1/2 teaspoon Worcestershire sauce
1/4 cup sour cream

## Cooking
1. Combine the ground venison with 2 tablespoons of the oil and the egg in a bowl. Mix, and shape into patties. Wash, dry, and slice the mushrooms and set aside.
2. Heat the last of the oil over medium-high heat, until the oil sizzles. Place the burger patties in the skillet. When the meat gets sizzling, turn the heat down to medium and cook about 3-4 minutes per side, or until all the pink is gone in the middle.
2. Meanwhile, in a second skillet, over medium-high heat, melt the butter until it sizzles and starts to get lightly browned, about 2 minutes. Add the mushrooms immediately. Shake the pan gently until the mushrooms are coated with the butter, then reduce the heat to low.
3. Add the beef bouillon, pepper, Worcestershire sauce, and sour cream and gently stir the sauce into the mushrooms. Pour over the burgers in the first skillet, and let it cook another 2 to 3 minutes spooning the sauce over the burgers several times. Serve hot, with Oven Fries or this Sweet Rice.

# Wild Sides: Sweet Rice
Serves 4-6

Yes, there's chicken bouillon, but that and the Walla Walla onion are what give this dish its deeply mellow sweetness. And despite the chicken, it goes well with venison burgers and sausage.

## Ingredients
1 sweet Walla Walla onion, sliced thin
2 tablespoons butter
2 cups uncooked rice
3 cups chicken bouillon
1 cup water

## Cooking
1. Sauté the onion in the butter over medium heat, until lightly golden. Stir the rice into the onion, and continue cooking until the rice starts to brown.
2. Add the bouillon and water, bring to a low boil, cover and reduce the heat to low. Cook about 30 minutes until all the rice has absorbed all the water.

# Pseudo Corn Dogs
Makes 8 or 16

I love corn dogs, and the closest I've ever come—in an easy-to-use recipe—is this one. Like all good recipes, this one can be made two ways: you can cut each crescent roll in half and wrap it around a tablespoon sized ball of the meat mixture, or shape the meat mixture into 8 thumb-shaped mini-sausages and roll a whole crescent roll around it, in the traditional crescent shape. The former gets fried, then baked to finish off the meat; the latter baked. Either way, they're a tasty snack.

## Ingredients
1 pound ground venison
1 egg, beaten
1 1/2 teaspoons dried leaf oregano
1 teaspoon garlic powder
1 tablespoon dried onion flakes
1/2 teaspoon red Tabasco sauce
1 teaspoon salt
1/2 teaspoon pepper
1 tube refrigerator crescent rolls

## Preparation
In a large bowl mix the venison, egg, oregano, garlic powder, Tabasco, salt and pepper thoroughly. Cover and refrigerate overnight.

## Cooking
1. Preheat the oven to 350°F. If you're frying, preheat the deep fryer to 375°F, and place a cookie sheet in the oven.
2. For the fried version: cut each crescent roll in half. Roll a tablespoon sized chunk of the meat mixture into the half roll, and pinch the dough closed. Fry until golden brown, and transfer to the cookie sheet. Bake 10 minutes and serve.
3. For the totally baked version: shape the meat mixture into 8 thumb-sized mini-sausages. Place each on a triangle of crescent dough, roll, and place on a cookie sheet. Bake 15 minutes and serve.

# Wild Sides: Curried Potato Salad
Serves 6-8

Are there ever enough potato salad recipes? I don't think so. And this one proves it.

## Ingredients
1 1/2 pounds potatoes
1/2 yellow onion, chopped
2 eggs
1/2 cup mayonnaise
2 tablespoons rice wine vinegar
1 teaspoon curry powder
8 green onions, chopped

## Cooking
1. Boil the potatoes until just fork-tender. (About 20 minutes for medium sized potatoes; more for bigger ones.) Boil the eggs. Cool both with running cold water, then chill 1-2 hours.
2. Chop the chilled potatoes and eggs into a large bowl with the onion. In a small bowl, combine the mayonnaise, vinegar, and curry powder. Gently toss the mayonnaise mixture and green onions into the potatoes. Cover, chill, and then serve.

# Easy Meaty Chili
## Serves 8

If you haven't discovered Rotel yet, you may want to buy an extra can (chopped tomatoes with lime and cilantro) for a delicious and easy tortilla dip. It adds a fresh Mexican flavor to the chili, but mixed with a jar of Cheese Whiz, makes an easy and delicious cold dip, and if you have access to a microwave, mix equal parts of Rotel with diced Velveeta, and zap it 20 to 30 seconds for a belly-warming corn chip dip--or even poured over toast for a quick pick-me up after a cold hunt. (Followed, of course, by hot canned peaches--please open the can before heating.)

## Ingredients
- 3 tablespoons oil, in all
- 1 yellow onion, chopped
- 3 cloves garlic, minced
- 1 1/2 teaspoons ground cumin
- 2 teaspoons dried leaf oregano
- 10 ounce can of Rotel tomatoes with lime and cilantro
- 1 pound ground venison
- 14.5 ounce can diced tomatoes
- 1 1/2 cups frozen corn, thawed
- 2 cups beef bouillon
- 10 ounces grated Monterey Jack cheese or sour cream

## Cooking
1. In a 3-4 quart Dutch oven, heat 2 tablespoons of the oil over medium-high heat. Add the onion and garlic and sauté until golden brown, then add the cumin and oregano and stir together. Add the Rotel and bring the pot back to a simmer.
2. Start a large skillet, also over medium-high heat and brown the ground venison in the last tablespoon of oil. When browned add to the Dutch oven.
3. Add the can of diced tomato, corn, and beef bouillon and bring the pot to a slow boil. Turn the heat to low and cover, cooking 45 minutes to an hour, minimum. As with all long cooking dishes, longer cooking makes chili better. And leftovers are always a treat the second day.
4. To serve, grate 2 to 3 tablespoons of cheese or drop a dollop of sour cream on the top.

## Wild Sides: Wrap It Up

If you think leftovers are boring, you need to try this. It's called an Indian Taco, and you run into them in most county fairs in the Western United States. What makes them different from a traditional taco is that instead of a corn tortilla, they're built on a chunk of freshly fried bread. Let's assume you ate half the chili at lunch: here's how to make 4 Indian Tacos.

Start the night before: thaw a loaf of frozen white bread in the fridge overnight. A couple of hours before you start cooking, set the bread out at room temperature, outside its bag, and let it double in size. Divide the risen loaf into 4 equal parts; press each round into a flat circle between your palms.

All that's left is the frying. In enough oil or shortening to rise about halfway up the bread round, fry each round over medium high heat on both sides until golden brown. Let them drain on paper towels.

When they're cool enough to handle, add some chili, grated cheese, sour cream, raw onions, salsa, whatever you want. Enjoy.

# Rib-Sticking Meat Loaf
Serves 4-6

I can never decide if I like my meat loaf better hot or cold. There's nothing like digging into a meat loaf hot, after smelling its tantalizing aroma for 30 minutes or more. But, then again, a meat loaf sandwich on hard roll, either standing in the kitchen, or sitting on a deer stand is hard to beat. Maybe we should just make two meat loaves at a time.

## Ingredients
1 14.5 ounce can diced tomatoes
1/2 cup sour cream
1 pound ground venison
1 egg
3/4 cup beef bouillon
1 tablespoon Worcestershire sauce
1/2 cup bread crumbs
3 tablespoons dried onion flakes
2 teaspoons dried leaf basil
1 teaspoon dried leaf thyme
1/2 teaspoon garlic powder
1/2 teaspoon celery salt
1 teaspoon salt
1/2 teaspoon pepper

## Cooking
1. Preheat the oven to 350°F. In a small bowl, combine the tomatoes and sour cream. Mix well and set aside.
2. In a large bowl, combine the rest of the ingredients. Mix well. Shape into a loaf about 1 1/2 to 1 3/4 inches high and place in a loaf pan or a cast iron skillet. Press the center of the loaf down to make a shallow bowl; starting by filling the bowl, pour all the tomato/sour cream sauce over loaf.
3. Bake uncovered for 60 minutes. Serve hot, with these simple Clean-Oven Onions, and baked potatoes with chives and sour cream.

## Wild Sides: Clean-Oven Onions

It's hard to say how many an onion feeds. I can make a dinner out of one nice red onion with a small elk steak on the side. John goes the other way: half an onion with a big steak. It's up to you, and simple to decide, but I wouldn't miss the opportunity to stick these onions in the oven with the meat loaf, as well as a potato for each person coming to dinner. All three will take about the same time in the oven. Way to save energy!

## Ingredients
2 whole red onions
2 tablespoons butter or margarine
1/2 teaspoon salt
1/4 teaspoon pepper

## Cooking
1. Preheat the oven to 350°F. Remove the outer dead or brittle layers of the onion, and trim off the root. Cut off the tops so you have a flat surface an inch or inch two in diameter to hold butter. Now, cut a deep x into that flat surface.
2. Wrap the onion in foil, and put 1 tablespoon of butter and the salt and pepper on top of each.
3. Close the foil and bake 45 to 60 minutes, or until tender. To serve, carefully open the foil, and slice thick or thin.

# Swedish Meatballs
Serves 4

Use your best tasting ground venison for these meatballs: they're creamy and rich but the taste is delicate. This sauce will fill your need for comfort food, but it has nowhere to hide a gamy animal.

## Ingredients
1/2 cup minced onion
6 tablespoons butter or margarine, in all
2/3 cup bread crumbs
1 1/3 cup milk, in all
3/8 teaspoon ground nutmeg
1/4 cup fresh minced parsley
1/4 teaspoon pepper
1 pound ground venison
3 tablespoons oil
1/2 cup boiling water
2 tablespoons flour
1 1/4 cup whipping cream
Egg noodles

## Cooking
1. Preheat the oven to 250°F. In a large skillet over medium heat, sauté the onions in 2 tablespoon of the butter until soft. Let cool. Combine the bread crumbs and 2/3 cup of the milk in a small bowl and let them soak about 5 minutes.
2. Add the onions to the bread/milk mixture, and add 1/4 teaspoon of the nutmeg, all the parsley, pepper and ground venison. Mix thoroughly by hand and shape into 2-inch balls.
3. In the skillet over medium heat, brown the meatballs in the rest of the butter and oil, a few at a time, transferring the browned meatballs to a plate in the oven.
4. When all the meatballs are browned, add the water to the pan drippings and simmer, stirring, for 5 minutes. Dissolve the flour in the last of the milk, and add the mixture to the pan. Add the cream and remaining nutmeg. Reduce the heat to a simmer, and continue cooking stirring constantly, until the gravy thickens.
5. Return the meatballs to the gravy, and let them cook another 1 to 2 minutes, spooning the sauce over them. Serve over egg noodles.

# Meatball Wedgies
Serves 4-6

It's a regional thing: whether you call them a hoagie, hero, or po' boy, this is a great way to build a sandwich. But, in my childhood neighborhood, it was wedgies, specifically meatball wedgies--Italian flavored meatballs stacked on a hard roll with lots of mozzarella and Parmesan cheese, and just enough tomato sauce to make it one of those all-time, all-occasion favorite dishes.

## Ingredients
2 pounds ground venison
4 eggs, beaten
2 cups breadcrumbs
4 cloves garlic, minced
1/2 cup chopped fresh parsley
1/2 cup chopped fresh sweet basil
1 teaspoon cracked fennel seed
1 teaspoon salt
1 teaspoon pepper
26-ounce bottle prepared marinara sauce
1 pound mozzarella, sliced
1 cup grated Parmesan cheese
4 hard rolls, about 6" long

## Cooking
1. Preheat the oven to 350°F. In a large bowl, combine the ground venison, eggs, breadcrumbs, garlic, parsley, basil, fennel, salt and pepper.
2. Roll into meatballs, about 1 tablespoon each, and arrange in a single layer on a baking pan, or large cast iron skillet. Pour the marinara sauce over them. Bake uncovered for 25 minutes. Turn on the broiler.
3. Split the hard rolls open, and lightly toast them under the broiler (on a cookie sheet 3 inches from the flame). Arrange the meatballs on the split open hard rolls, pour the sauce over the meatballs, and top with the mozzarella and Parmesan cheese.
4. Place the assembled wedgies under the broiler, and heat until the cheese bubbles and browns slightly, about 3-4 minutes. Serve hot, with chips and a nice cold beer.

# Mexican Lasagna
Serves 6

An easier variation on the Italian classic. If you can brown burger and open a jar, you can make this dish. But Mexican Lasagna isn't just delicious; it adjusts to fit every level of heat. Make it as written here and it's a great meal for middle-of-the-roaders; use hotter salsa or add chili pepper to the mixture and you'll have a much hotter dish. And you don't have to go beyond step one: pour the results of step one into a bowl, add a little cheese and sour cream, and you have an easy chili some Saturday afternoon. It's up to you. By the way, that Chipotle Tabasco sauce isn't nearly as fiery as the red Tabasco; use more if you want.

## Ingredients
2 tablespoons oil
2 pounds ground venison
2 bottles mild salsa (15 ounce each)
1 tablespoon Chipotle Tabasco sauce
2 cans (15 ounce) pinto beans, drained and rinsed
4 large (7") corn tortillas
16 ounces Monterey Jack cheese, grated or sliced

## Cooking
1. Preheat the oven to 350°F. In a large skillet brown the burger in the oil over medium-high heat. Stir in the chunky salsa and Chipotle Tabasco sauce. Turn the heat off.
2. Layer the lasagna in a 9x13 baking pan: first, half of the meat/tomato mixture, sprinkled with half of the beans; then two tortillas across the dish; then half of the cheese. Repeat, and finish with the cheese. Cover with foil, and bake 30 minutes. (Uncover and broil for another 5 minutes to get a nice crisp brown crust.) Serve hot with dollops of sour cream, if desired.

# Baked Ziti
Serves 6-8

There's something that happens to pasta when you bake it this way, even if you cheat and use a bottled sauce instead of homemade. (In a pinch, my favorite bottled sauce is Prego Traditional Pasta Sauce.) However you make it, this is a great stick-to-your-ribs winter dish that is the very definition of comfort food. Feel free to substitute homemade Italian Sausage for the meatballs. If you have some already made up in the freezer, it will be delicious, and a lot faster.

## Ingredients
1 tablespoon oil
1 large yellow onion, sliced
3 cloves garlic, minced
2 tablespoons medium dry sherry
2 tablespoons sugar
1 tablespoon dried leaf oregano
1/4 teaspoon pepper
28 ounce can chopped tomatoes
15 ounce can tomato sauce
2 pounds ground venison
5 eggs, beaten
2 cups Italian flavored breadcrumbs
1 teaspoon salt
1/2 teaspoon pepper
1/8 teaspoon red pepper flakes
1 cup grated Parmesan cheese, in all
16 ounce box ziti or any tube pasta

## Cooking
1. Preheat the oven to 350°F. Heat the oil over medium-high heat in a large skillet. Add the onion and garlic and turn the heat down to medium low. Cook until the onion is tender. Add the sherry, sugar, oregano and pepper and stir into the onion. Cook until the onions start to sizzle again.
2. Add the tomatoes and tomato sauce, raise the heat to high. When the sauce starts bubbling again, lower the heat to a low simmer and cook uncovered for 30 minutes.
3. While the sauce cooks, mix the ground venison, eggs, breadcrumbs, salt, black and red peppers, and 1/2 cup of the Parmesan cheese. Shape into meatballs about 2-inches in diameter.
3. Cook the ziti according to package directions and drain. Pour the ziti into a 13x9-inch baking dish. Stir the sauce into the ziti. Nestle the meatballs into the pasta and sauce. Top with the rest of the Parmesan cheese. Cover the dish tightly with foil.
4. Bake for 30 minutes. Remove the foil and bake another 30 minutes uncovered. Serve immediately with green salad.

# Meatballs And Spaghetti
Serves 4-6

Mixing your own Italian sausage with plain ground venison, turns America's favorite comfort food into an easy, breezy dinner. If you don't have any of your own homemade Italian sausage, you can also substitute the meatball ingredients from the Wedgie recipe or the Baked Ziti a few pages back. And, of course you can also use commercial Italian sausage, and commercial bottled marinara sauce. But this is pretty easy just as it's written, too.

## Ingredients
8 ounces Italian sausage
8 ounces ground venison
3 tablespoons olive or grape seed oil, in all
1 medium yellow onion, sliced
5 cloves garlic, minced
1 tablespoon dried leaf sweet basil
1 teaspoon dried leaf winter savory
1/2 cup medium dry sherry
2 cans (14.5 ounces each) diced tomatoes
1 pound spaghetti or other pasta
Grated Parmesan cheese

## Cooking
1. Combine the sausage and ground venison, and shape into 1" round meatballs.
2. In a 4 to 5-quart Dutch oven, heat half the oil over medium-high heat. When the oil starts sizzling, add the meat balls a few at a time, without crowding in the pan, and lightly brown them. Turn gently to brown them all around, without their breaking apart. Transfer the meatballs to a heated platter and cover with foil.
3. Add the remaining oil, and sauté the onions and garlic over medium heat, until golden brown. Add the basil and savory, and stir together. When the aroma of herbs starts filling the room, add the sherry, stirring up all the caramelized bits from the bottom of the pan. Let the sherry reduce by about half, and then add the tomatoes.
4. Bring the sauce back to a slow simmer, return the meatballs to the pot, and let it all cook about 20 minutes, as you boil the spaghetti.
5. Serve with lots of Parmesan cheese and a green salad.

****For those watching their fat, you can also just add the raw meatballs to the simmering sauce, à la the Mexican Meatball Soup. They'll cook in 8-10 minutes. The rest of the cooking is just to let the flavors mix. And to vary the sauce now and then, consider adding one or two fire roasted red peppers. They add a lot of flavor, and come prepared, in a jar, easy to use.

# 1-2-3 Tortilla Pie
Serves 4-6

This may look like a lot of ingredients, but if you can brown burger and open a can, you won't go hungry. The best part of this recipe, however, is that it includes one of my other favorite comfort foods--creamed corn. The creamed corn makes this dish really simple, since it's what holds it together and is richer tasting than plain corn starch. And in case you don't have enough burger recipes, there are two variations on the theme.

## Ingredients
1 1/2 pounds ground venison
1 onion, sliced thin
3 tablespoons oil
2/3 cup catsup
10 ounce can mild Rotel
4 tortillas, quartered
1 cup grated Mozzarella cheese
15 ounce can creamed corn
1 1/2 tablespoons corn meal
1 tablespoon chipotle Tabasco sauce

## Cooking
1. Preheat the oven to 350°F. In a large skillet, over medium heat brown the ground venison and onion in the oil just until the pink is out of the meat. Add the catsup and Rotel and stir.
2. Arrange the tortilla pieces in the bottom of a 9x9" square baking dish. Pour the meat/Rotel mixture over them, and cover with the grated cheese. Combine the creamed corn, cornmeal, and Tabasco sauce until well blended and spread it evenly across the top.
3. Cover the baking dish with foil, and bake 45 minutes covered, then 15 more uncovered. Serve hot.

## Wild Variations: Nacho Chips

This spiced burger mix also makes a lazy man's (or woman's) nacho snack for 4. Go ahead and do step one, browning the burger, and adding the catsup and Rotel.

Then toss a few tortilla chips on 4 plates, divide the seasoned burger and spoon it on top. Now, sprinkle with grated Jack cheese, set it under the broiler until the cheese starts to sizzle. Remove, and add the cold stuff: a bit of sour cream and sliced olives; fresh salsa and even Tabasco sauce if you want. But my guess is that the Rotel will have enough heat for most people.

## Wild Variations: Taco Salad

Need something on a hot summer day that doesn't heat you up? Take the spiced burger mix from step one of the tortilla pie: after it's cooled to room temperature, spoon it over some corn chips and top with shredded lettuce, sliced tomato, olives, and jalapeno pepper, and serve it with a bit of sour cream or ranch dressing. If you need more heat, add a little chipotle tabasco sauce to the sour cream or ranch dressing and pour it over the top. No need to go bland just because the temperature is soaring.

# Mexican Meatballs and Rice
Serves 4

Make a Mexican-style wedgie sandwich out of these meatballs and sauce (just add Monterey Jack cheese instead of mozzarella and Parmesan) or make this more formal dinner with rice. Either way these meatballs are as tasty as the traditional Italian style. And you can control the heat with the enchilada sauce you choose: mild to hot.

## Ingredients
1 pound ground venison
2 eggs, beaten
1 cup bread crumbs
1/4 cup loosely packed chopped fresh cilantro
1/4 teaspoon garlic powder
1 teaspoon salt
1/2 teaspoon pepper
19 ounce can green enchilada sauce
3 cups cooked rice (from 1 cup raw)

## Cooking
1. Preheat the oven to 350°F. Combine the ground venison with the eggs, bread crumbs, cilantro, garlic powder, salt, and pepper.
2. Shape into 1 1/2-inch diameter meatballs and arrange on a baking pan or cast iron skillet in a single layer. (You should have about 16.) Pour the enchilada sauce over the top and bake 25 minutes, uncovered.
3. When done, pour over the rice and serve.

# Easy Mexican Albondigas

Mexican meatball soup, like hoagies and wedgies vary from region to region, but this one is the one I like best. It uses the meatballs from the previous recipe, in a pot of doctored up canned beef bouillon. It doesn't get any easier than that.

## Ingredients
1 pound Mexican meatballs
3 cans beef broth, 14 1/2 ounces each
1 ripe tomato, diced
1 clove garlic, minced
1/2 teaspoon ground cumin
1 green onion, chopped

## Cooking
1. Pour the beef broth into a large pot and bring to a boil over high heat.
2. Add the meatballs to the pot, gently, a few at a time, letting the pot come back to a boil, with each addition, until all of them are in the pot. Add the tomato and garlic, lower the heat to a simmer and cover the pot.
3. Simmer about 15 minutes, and serve with the green onion, fresh, on top.

# Smoked Meat Loaf

I've found that the only way to get the results I want for this meat loaf--delicious and juicy--is to use a water smoker. They're a tall, domed cooker, with a reservoir for water inside. (Of course you can put any liquid you want in the reservoir, but water is enough to provide the gentle moist heat that makes this dish one of the favorites among my friends.)

## Ingredients
3 chunks hickory
1 cup chopped onion
1/2 cup chopped green bell pepper
4 cloves garlic, minced
1 tablespoon oil
1/2 teaspoon ground cumin
1/2 teaspoon salt
1 teaspoon black pepper
1 1/2 pounds ground venison
1/4 cup sour cream
1 egg
1 cup bread crumbs
1/2 cup cornmeal
2 tablespoons Worcestershire sauce
1 tablespoon green jalapeno pepper sauce
1 teaspoon beef bouillon granules
1/2 cup hot water

## Preparation
1. Two hours before you want to start cooking, place the hickory chunks in water. In a skillet over medium heat, sauté the onion, peppers, and garlic in oil until wilted. Stir in the cumin, salt, and pepper and continue to cook unto the vegetables are lightly browned. Transfer them to a large bowl.
2. Add the burger, sour cream, egg, bread crumbs, corn meal, Worcestershire sauce, and green pepper sauce to the browned vegetables and mix. Dissolve the bouillon granules in the water and add that to the meat loaf, too. Mix thoroughly with your hands and press into a metal loaf pan.

## Cooking
1. Assemble the water smoker with the soaked hickory chips at the bottom and the reservoir 2/3 full of water, and preheat it to low-medium setting (220 to 240°F).
2. Place the meat loaf pan in the center of the cooking rack. Cover the cooker. Let the meat loaf cook for 60 minutes, until it has shrunk away from the sides of the pan.
3. Place a length of foil over the top, and turn the meat loaf out into your hand (wearing a good hot mitt for protection). Gently invert the meat loaf back onto the cooking grate, so it's now upright again, on the foil, but without the loaf pan. (Before you invert the meat loaf, check that your reservoir is still about 1/2 full or more. Add more water if necessary.)
4. Cover the cooker and let it cook another 60 minutes. (If you like, check the meat loaf with a meat thermometer: finished temperature should be 165°F.)
5. Lift the meat loaf carefully off the rack, with a pair of spatulas and a plate handy to slide underneath it. Let sit 5 minutes, then slice.
6. Serve with the Chilled Broccoli Salad.

# Tough & Tougher
## Sausage & Jerky

# Breakfast Sausage
Makes 1 1/2 pounds

Grind the side pork and venison separately. Slightly frozen meats will grind more easily and retain more moisture--especially the side pork. And keep the mix cool; if you're interrupted, refrigerate everything--including the grinder head--in resealable plastic bags. And, feel free to double or triple the recipe. If you want to make more sausage than that, make a new triple batch rather than putting all your eggs--so to speak--in one casing. Something happens to the spice proportions when you go much beyond tripling a recipe.

## Ingredients
3/4 pound ground venison
3/4 pound ground side pork
1 3/4 teaspoons salt
1/2 teaspoon coarse ground black pepper
1/2 teaspoon red pepper flakes
1 teaspoon Tabasco brand chipotle pepper sauce
1 tablespoon dried onion flakes
1/2 teaspoon ground sage
1/2 teaspoon dried leaf thyme
3/4 teaspoon ground allspice

## Preparation
1. Mix all the ingredients together with your hands. Cover and refrigerate for 24 hours, and then test for flavor in the microwave or pan. Details at right.
2. Once you've corrected the seasoning, double wrap the sausage for the freezer, or refrigerate until using. It will keep in the refrigerator for 3-4 days; in the freezer for up to 2 months.

## Cooking
1. Shape into patties, and cook in a fry pan, with about 2 tablespoons of oil, until all the pink is gone.
2. Serve with eggs and biscuits or make the Second Breakfast that follows.

## Tips & Tactics: Taste Testing Safely
Keeping in mind that it takes 12-24 hours for flavors to fully develop in any recipe—including sausage—it's a good idea to let your mix sit in the fridge overnight before you taste it. More important though, is that you not taste raw sausage.

So mix your sausage, refrigerate it overnight well-covered, then the next day roll a ball of sausage about 1-inch in diameter, place it in a microwave safe cup, and microwave on high for about 30 seconds, or until all the pink is gone. Taste your sausage, and correct the seasonings. More salt, more chipotle pepper sauce, whatever you think needs more presence. Then check it again, by cooking in the microwave.

If you don't own a microwave, flatten the test ball into a patty, and cook it in a skillet until all the pink is gone. Never, never, never eat raw sausage, not even the smallest amount. No matter how careful you've been, and how certified your pork and clean your venison. Stuff happens.

# Second Breakfast-in-a-Pot
Serves 4-6 hungry people

Take that Breakfast Sausage you just made and make yourself a breakfast that will serve a crowd. It will fill your belly and keep you going whether you're hunting, cutting firewood or vegging out in front of the TV.

## Ingredients
1 1/2 pounds Breakfast Sausage
1 tablespoon oil
1 medium onion, chopped
32 ounce bag frozen hash browns, thawed
1/2 teaspoon salt
1/2 teaspoon garlic salt
16 ounce jar Classico Alfredo sauce
8 eggs
1 pound (4 cups) bag grated mozzarella cheese
1/2 cup grated Parmesan cheese

## Cooking
1. Preheat the oven to 300°F. Brown the sausage in oil over medium-high heat in a 3-quart Dutch oven. Add the onion and brown it in the sausage and drippings until all the juices are absorbed. Add the hash browns, salt, garlic salt, and bottled Classico Alfredo sauce. Toss gently.
2. Cover the Dutch oven, and place in the oven. Bake 25 minutes; uncover and break the eggs (in a single layer) across the top of the dish. Cover and bake another 10 minutes until the eggs are done. Sprinkle both grated cheeses on top, and serve.

# Christmas Chorizo

Makes 1 pound

This is the basic one-pound recipe. Once you adapt it to your tastes, you can double or triple the recipe at will. Case these sausages and throw them on the grill, or cook them un-cased in a skillet. Chorizo is versatile: the Southwestern Egg Rolls on the facing page make a tasty snack, and the Christmas Chorizo Rollups in The Middle section of this book are a treat on special occasions. So why is it called Christmas chorizo? Party because the jalapenos and red peppers make it pretty festive, but also because we often make sausage at Christmas and share it with our friends. Last holiday season, we used it in our New Year's Day Hoppin' John instead of traditional Cajun sausage and it was wonderful. (To try that, omit the bay leaves, use 2 red bell peppers, and add black beans instead of black-eyed peas, in the Cajun variation on page 175.)

## Ingredients

8 ounces ground venison
8 ounces ground side pork
1 quarter of a medium yellow onion
1 tablespoon bottled roasted red pepper
4 cloves garlic
1 teaspoon canned mild jalapenos
1 tablespoon smoked chipotle Tabasco sauce
1/3 cup minced fresh cilantro
3 tablespoons cold water
1 1/2 teaspoons ground cumin
1/2 teaspoon salt

## Preparation

1. Mix the ground venison and ground pork together with your hands. Purée the rest of the ingredients together in a food processor and mix into the pork/venison thoroughly. Cover and refrigerate for 24 hours, and then test for flavor, cooking a small amount in the microwave to sample it.
2. Once you've corrected the seasoning (more salt, more jalapeno, hotter jalapeno), double wrap the sausage for the freezer, or refrigerate until using. It will keep in the refrigerator for 3-4 days; in the freezer for up to 2 months.

## Cooking

1. Shape into patties, and cook in a fry pan, with about 2 tablespoons of oil, turning once, until all the pink is gone.
2. Serve with fried eggs, prepared refried beans, Mexican Rice or in the Southwestern Egg Rolls that follow. And don't forget the Christmas Chorizo Rollups.

# Southwestern Egg Rolls

Makes 8 egg rolls

Take a pound of your uncased chorizo and a package of egg roll wrappers and what do you have? A multi-cultural, mouth-filling snack for Super Bowl Sunday or any time you have the hungries. Feel free to vary the ingredients: sour cream, nopalitos, refried beans, corn, whatever strikes your fancy, but don't leave out the chorizo.

## Ingredients
1 pound chorizo
2 tablespoons corn starch
2 tablespoons cold water
15 ounce can black beans, drained
1 cup fresh salsa
8 egg roll wrappers

## Cooking
1. Break up and lightly brown the chorizo in a skillet over medium heat. Preheat a deep fryer to 375°F. Stir the corn starch into the cold water.
2. Lay out each egg roll wrapper one at a time, and spoon 2 tablespoons each of the beans, salsa, and cooked chorizo in the middle of the wrapper. Wipe some of the cornstarch solution on all four edges of the wrapper.
3. Roll one end up and over the filling, tuck in the ends, and finish rolling. Carefully lower into the hot oil, and cook about 4 minutes until golden brown.
4. Serve hot with more salsa, or ranch dressing.

# Polish Sausage
Makes 1 pound

Sometimes sausage is a very simple process with few, very common ingredients. That's true of this one, but the caraway seed makes it a zesty and bright variation of the sausage theme. The real question is do you want to case it or simply shape into patties.

## Ingredients
1/2 pound side pork, ground
1/2 pound venison, ground
1 teaspoon sugar
1 teaspoon dried sage leaves
1/2 teaspoon dried thyme leaves
1 1/4 teaspoon salt
1/2 teaspoon coarse ground black pepper
1 teaspoon caraway seeds

## Preparation
1. In a large bowl, combine the ground meats and the spices, mixing thoroughly by hand. Case, or if you don't have any cases, shape into patties.
2. To store for later cooking, double wrap in plastic wrap and freezer paper. The sausage will keep in the freezer for up to 2 months.

## Cooking
1. Cased on the stove: Place the cased sausages into a frying pan, and pour enough water into the pan to rise halfway up the sausages. Bring to a low boil, and lower the heat. Simmer until the water has all evaporated, about 30 minutes. Serve.
2. Cased on the grill: Preheat the grill to medium, and lightly oil each cased sausage before placing on the grill. Cook until all the pink is gone, turning 4-5 times to prevent burning.
3. Patties: Shape the sausage into patties as you would your burgers, then cook on the grill, or in a skillet, until all the pink is gone. Be sure to brush a little oil on the grill before cooking the patties; 1 tablespoon of oil will suffice in the skillet.
4. Serve hot with Josh's Sweet Potato Salad.

# Wild Sides: Josh's Sweet Potato Salad

Josh doesn't make this salad anymore since her doctor scared the fat out of her diet. But it's a great recipe, and I know she has dreams of being able to indulge again someday. In the meantime, there's more for us.

## Ingredients
6 sweet potatoes, boiled
6 hard-boiled eggs
1 cup chopped onions
1 cup chopped celery
1 cup mayonnaise
Pinch of cinnamon
1 teaspoon salt
1/2 teaspoon pepper

## Cooking
1. Dice the potatoes and eggs and toss in a large bowl with the onions, celery, mayonnaise, and cinnamon, salt, and pepper.
2. Chill and serve.

## Butte, America Sausage
Makes 1 pound

Mace is a fairly common spice, ground from the outside shell of nutmeg. My grocery store 2 blocks away doesn't carry it, but when I go to the big city (25,000 people 30 minutes away) it's as common as thyme. And there are usually antelope out on the sage brush flats as we drive by so it is a trip worth making. So is this sausage.

### Ingredients
- 1/2 pound side pork, ground
- 1/2 pound venison, ground
- 1 teaspoon sugar
- 1 teaspoon celery salt
- 1/2 teaspoon garlic salt
- 1 teaspoon dried sage leaves
- 1/2 teaspoon dried thyme leaves
- 1/2 teaspoon ground mace
- 1 1/8 teaspoon salt
- 1 1/4 teaspoon coarse ground black pepper

### Preparation
1. In a large bowl, combine the ground meats and the spices, mixing thoroughly by hand. Case, or if you don't have any cases, shape into patties.
2. To store for later cooking, double wrap in plastic wrap and freezer paper. The sausage will keep in the freezer for up to 2 months.

### Cooking
1. Cased on the stove: place the cased sausages into a frying pan, and pour enough water into the pan to rise halfway up the sausages. Bring to a low boil, and lower the heat. Simmer until the water has all evaporated or about 30 minutes
2. Cased on the grill: Preheat the grill to medium, and lightly oil each cased sausage before placing on the grill. Cook until all the pink is gone, turning 4-5 times to prevent burning.
3. Patties: Shape the sausage into patties as you would your burgers, then cook on the grill, or in a skillet, until all the pink is gone. Be sure to brush a little oil on the grill before cooking the patties; 1 tablespoon of oil will suffice in the skillet.
4. Serve with Potato Pancakes or Two-Can Baked Beans; or on a hard roll with mustard and relish and a side of Sweet and Sour Refrigerator Pickles.

## Wild Sides: Potato Pancakes
Makes 12 4-inch pancakes

Spoon about 1/4 cup of batter into the skillet for each cake, and while we're at it, please consider serving potato pancakes with your eggs and breakfast sausage in the morning. They're a dramatic change from 'normal.'

### Ingredients
- 24 ounce bag frozen hash browns, thawed
- 2 eggs
- 3/4 cup sour cream
- 1/4 cup flour
- 1 cup chopped onion (about 1/2 medium onion)
- 1 1/2 teaspoons salt
- 1 teaspoon pepper
- 1 apple, peeled, cored and grated
- 1/2 teaspoon ground clove
- 1/4 cup oil or margarine (or half each)

### Cooking
1. Combine all the ingredients except the oil in a large bowl, and stir together. Preheat the oven to 200°F and set a plate in the center.
2. Heat 1-2 tablespoons butter/oil in a skillet for each batch and brown the cakes on both sides over high heat, about 7 minutes. Keep warm in the oven; serve hot.

# Un-Smoked Smoky Sausage
Makes 1 pound

Smoked paprika is a variation on the sweet paprika found in most grocery stores. It adds a gentle, earthy smoke flavor to this mix. If you have a hard time finding it, try a health food store; they usually carry a wider variety of spices than grocery chains.

## Ingredients
1/2 pound side pork, ground
1/2 pound venison, ground
1 teaspoon sugar
1 teaspoon dried sage leaves
1/2 teaspoon dried thyme leaves
2 teaspoons salt
1/2 teaspoon coarse ground black pepper
2 teaspoon smoked paprika

## Preparation
1. In a large bowl, combine the ground meats and the spices, mixing thoroughly by hand. Case, or if you don't have any cases, shape into patties.
2. To store for later cooking, double wrap in plastic wrap and freezer paper. The sausage will keep in the freezer for up to 2 months.

## Cooking
1. Cased on the stove: place the cased sausages into a frying pan, and pour enough water into the pan to rise halfway up the sausages. Bring to a low boil on high, then lower the heat and simmer until the water has all evaporated (about 30 minutes).
2. Cased on the grill: Preheat the grill to medium, and lightly oil each cased sausage before placing on the grill. Cook until all the pink is gone, turning 4-5 times to prevent burning.
3. Patties: Shape the sausage into patties as you would your burgers, then cook on the grill, or in a skillet, until all the pink is gone. Be sure to brush a little oil on the grill before cooking the patties; 1 tablespoon of oil will suffice in the skillet.
4. Serve with potato salad in summer; Super Creamy Mac & Cheese or this Braised Red Cabbage in winter.

# Wild Sides: Braised Red Cabbage
Serves 4

## Ingredients
4 slices bacon, chopped
1 medium head red cabbage
1/4 cup apple cider vinegar
3 tablespoons brown sugar
2 tablespoons red currant jelly
1/2 teaspoon salt

## Cooking
1. In a large skillet, brown the bacon lightly, over medium heat. Add the sliced red cabbage and stir it into the pan drippings.
2. In a large bowl combine the vinegar, brown sugar, jelly, and salt. Set aside.
3. When the cabbage has reduced in size by about half, stir the vinegar mixture into it. Reduce the heat to medium-low, cover the skillet and let the cabbage cook 15-20 minutes more for crisp cabbage.

# Easy Italian Sausage
Makes 1 pound

Make this up and put it in your freezer. Then next time you start a pot of beef-based soup or stew, or start your favorite spaghetti sauce--add some of this delicious Italian sausage. It will spark up the most routine Wednesday night dinners. Don't make marinara from scratch? This sausage will make that bottled sauce sing like Pavarotti. Just roll the sausage into 1-inch diameter balls, and drop it into the sauce--while it's simmering in a saucepan, that is. The meatballs will cook in 10 to 15 minutes and you'll look like a culinary luminary. Really.

## Ingredients
1/2 pound ground venison
1/2 pound ground side pork
2 teaspoons dried onion flakes
1 teaspoon dried leaf basil
1 teaspoon whole fennel seeds, crushed
1 teaspoon salt
1/4 teaspoon garlic salt
1/2 teaspoon coarse ground black pepper

## Preparation
1. In a large bowl, combine the ground meats and the spices, mixing thoroughly by hand. (If you don't have a pestle for crushing the fennel seeds, put them in a plastic bag and roll a wine bottle across them until you can smell the fennel.) Case the sausage or shape into patties.
2. To store for later cooking, double wrap in plastic wrap and freezer paper. The sausage will keep in the freezer for up to 2 months.

## Cooking
1. Cased sausage indoors: Place the cased sausages into a frying pan, and pour enough water into the pan to rise halfway up the sausages. Bring to a low boil, and lower the heat. Simmer until the water has all evaporated or about 30 minutes.
2. Cased sausage on the grill: Preheat the grill to medium, and lightly oil each cased sausage before placing on the grill. Cook until all the pink is gone, turning 4-5 times to prevent burning.
3. Patties: Shape the sausage into patties as you would your burgers, then cook on the grill, or in a skillet, until all the pink is gone. Be sure to brush a little oil on the grill before cooking the patties; 1 tablespoon of oil will suffice in the skillet.
4. To add to tomato sauce or Alfredo, bring the sauce to a simmer, then add the sausage. (Shape them into balls small enough to be completely submerged in the sauce--or use a smaller saucepan to deepen the level of the sauce.)

## Brats
Makes 1 pound

I used to use pork shoulder for sausage recipes, but these days pork shoulder is leaner than it was only 15 years ago. I've found equal parts of ground venison and side pork provide the that creamy, melt in your mouth flavor that used to get with shoulder. But this is still a pretty lean sausage. If you want the fat dripping down your arms, up the ratio of side pork to venison. (Side pork is uncured bacon--and mostly fat with some waves of meat in it.)

### Ingredients
- 1/2 pound ground venison
- 1/2 pound ground side pork
- 1 teaspoon sugar
- 1 teaspoon dried sage leaves
- 1/2 teaspoon dried thyme leaves
- 1 1/4 teaspoons salt
- 1/2 teaspoon coarse ground black pepper

### Preparation
1. In a large bowl, combine the ground meats and the spices, mixing thoroughly by hand. Case, or if you don't have any cases, shape into patties.
2. To store for later cooking, double wrap in plastic wrap and freezer paper. The sausage will keep in the freezer for up to 2 months.

### Cooking
1. Cased on the stove: place the cased sausages into a frying pan, and pour enough water into the pan to rise halfway up the sausages. Bring to a low boil, and lower the heat. Simmer until the water has all evaporated or about 30 minutes.
2. Cased on the grill: Preheat the grill to medium, and lightly oil each cased sausage before placing on the grill. Cook until all the pink is gone, turning 4-5 times to prevent burning.
3. Patties: Shape the sausage into patties as you would your burgers, then cook on the grill, or in a skillet, until all the pink is gone. Be sure to brush a little oil on the grill before cooking the patties; 1 tablespoon of oil will suffice in the skillet.
4. Serve with Potato Pancakes and a side of Easy Mustard Pickles.

## Wild Sides: Easy Refrigerator Mustard Pickle
Makes 2 quarts

Here's a variation on the sweet and sour pickle earlier in these pages. This one takes a bit longer for the flavor to develop, but once the mustard seeds bloom, you'll be amazed at the zing of such a simple recipe.

### Ingredients
- 2 cups apple cider vinegar
- 2 cups sugar
- 2 tablespoons whole mustard seed
- 3 large cucumbers (about 3 pounds)

### Preparation
1. Get three quart jars clean and ready to use. In the first jar measure out the sugar and vinegar, and cover the jar tightly. Shake the jar, then let it sit on the counter. Repeat until the sugar has dissolved, about ten minutes and three shakes. Add the mustard seed.
2. In the meantime, slice the cucumbers and stuff them into the other two jars. When the sugar has dissolved totally, pour it over the sliced cucumbers. Close both jars tightly and chill at least 5 days before serving. That allows the mustard seed flavor to develop fully.

# Brats-in-a-Pot-Soup
Serves 8

Too cold to go out and light the grill? Brats make a flavorful base for any soup (as do the Polish, Butte, and Un-Smoked Smoky sausage that precede it). This is a traditional meat and potato stick-to-your-ribs soup that is perfect for cold winter nights, and while it's made here with the brats, feel free to substitute any of the above mentioned sausages. (By the way, for soups, the sausage doesn't need to be cased; and you can always substitute sour cream for the sprinkle of chives at the end, for cold winter nights.)

## Ingredients
5 tablespoons oil, in all
2 pounds brats, sliced 1 inch thick
1 medium onion, sliced thick
1 quart water
1 tablespoon beef bouillon granules (or beef base)
3 cups chopped potato
1 cup frozen corn
1/4 cup red currant jelly
2 tablespoons chopped chives (optional)

## Cooking
1. In a 5 quart Dutch oven, brown the brats in 2 tablespoons of the oil over medium heat. Transfer to a warm plate when browned. Add the rest of the oil to the pan and brown the onions until golden. Return the brats to the pot.
2. Add the water, beef bouillon, potato, corn, and jelly to the pot. Bring to a low boil, then turn down to simmer, and simmer about one hour. Sprinkle the chives over each serving; serve with dinner rolls.

# Cajun Sausage

Makes 1 pound

I'd suggest adding the cayenne pepper gradually until you find your comfort level because, while this sausage is delicious at my house, my cayenne might be milder--or hotter--than the brand you purchase. Too little is easily corrected, but once the cayenne gets too hot, you're committed to diluting it with more of everything else. Start with half, let it sit 12 to 24 hours, then adjust. When you're done, shape into patties, or case it, for grilling or frying, or add it to one-dish meals, like the Hoppin' John that follows.

## Ingredients
8 ounces ground venison
8 ounces ground side pork
1 teaspoon sweet paprika
1 teaspoon garlic salt
1 teaspoon dried leaf thyme
1 teaspoon dried leaf oregano
1 teaspoon onion powder
1/2 teaspoon dry mustard
1/4 teaspoon cayenne pepper
1/4 teaspoon white pepper

## Preparation
1. In a large bowl, combine the ground meats and the spices, mixing thoroughly by hand. Case, or shape into patties.
2. To store for later cooking, double wrap in plastic wrap and freezer paper. The sausage will keep in the freezer for up to 2 months.

## Cooking
1. Cased on the stove: Place the cased sausages into a frying pan, and pour enough water into the pan to rise halfway up the sausages. Bring to a low boil, and lower the heat. Simmer until the water has all evaporated or about 30 minutes.
2. Cased on the grill: Preheat the grill to medium, and lightly oil each cased sausage before placing on the grill. Cook until all the pink is gone, turning 4-5 times to prevent burning.
3. Patties: Shape the sausage into patties as you would your burgers, then cook on the grill, or in a skillet, until all the pink is gone. Be sure to brush a little oil on the grill before cooking the patty so they don't stick; 1 tablespoon of oil will suffice in the skillet.

# Hoppin' John
Serves 6

A New Year's Eve good luck tradition in part of the south, John and I make Hoppin' John every year just because it tastes great. If you don't have any Cajun sausage you can use bacon, but the sausage is easy to make, doesn't require casing, and adds a more complex flavor to the pot. Besides, you were looking for another way to use venison burger, weren't you?

## Ingredients
1 pound Cajun sausage
2 tablespoons oil
1 medium yellow onion, chopped
1 red or green bell pepper, chopped
1 clove garlic, minced
2 cups hot water
2 bay leaves
1 teaspoon salt
1/4 teaspoon cayenne pepper
1/4 teaspoon black pepper
2 15 ounce cans black-eyed peas, drained and rinsed
3 cups cooked rice

## Cooking
1. Brown the sausage in the oil over medium heat. Add the onion, green pepper, and garlic and sauté them until the onion is tender, 6-8 minutes.
2. Add the water, bay leaves, salt, both cayenne and black peppers, and black-eyed peas. Bring the pot back to a low (gentle) boil over high heat, reduce to low heat, cover, and simmer 40-50 minutes.
3. Remove the bay leaves, stir in the rice, and continue simmering another 10 minutes until all the liquid has been absorbed. Serve hot, with corn bread or garlic toast.

# Oven Salami
Makes two 8-inch salamis

     Make as much salami as you want, but make it up 2-4 pounds at a time; more than that tends to throw off the spice to meat ratio. (Another mystery from the wonderful world of meat.) And if you do multiply the recipe, keep the ratio of Morton's Tender Quick to meat consistent: 1 tablespoon per pound of fresh meat/suet.

## Ingredients
8 ounces beef suet
8 ounces ground venison
1 tablespoon Morton's Tender Quick
1 teaspoon dried basil flakes
1 teaspoon minced garlic (about 2 cloves)
1 teaspoon sugar
1/2 teaspoon white peppercorns, cracked
1/2 teaspoon dried sage leaf
1/2 teaspoon dried red pepper flakes
1/4 cup cold water

## Preparation
1. Grind the beef suet and venison through a large plate of your grinder. Once ground, add the Morton's Tender Quick to the ground meat/suet.
2. Add the rest of the ingredients and mix thoroughly. Place in a resealable plastic bag, seal, and refrigerate overnight.

## Cooking
1. Preheat the oven to 200°F. Before you cook the salami, do a taste test in the microwave: a 1-inch ball in a coffee mug (to prevent splatters) on high for 30 to 45 seconds or until all the pink is gone. Adjust the spices if necessary.
2. Lay a length of plastic wrap on the counter. Center an 8 ounce ball of salami mix on the plastic wrap and roll it into the plastic wrap, stretching the salami mix into a 2-inch diameter tube. Round off the ends, and carefully place on a baking pan (with a 1/2" lip to catch the grease), removing the plastic wrap as you do so. Repeat, until you've used all the meat or the baking pan is full, being sure to leave at least an inch of space between salamis. Cook for about 5 hours.
3. When done, transfer (with kitchen tongs) to a cake cooling rack with paper towels beneath. When cool, slice off an end. The meat will be red (from the nitrates) but not pink in the middle. If it's pink or feels mushy in the center after cooling, cook it until the pink is gone. Slice thin or thick for sandwiches, or on crackers for a fast nibble.

****2 level cups equals 1 pound of ground meat
****Variations on the recipe: Substitute red wine for the cold water to give it a more Genoa salami-like flavor. Or, for those who like heat, double or triple the red pepper flakes.

# Smoked Fajita Jerky

About 6 ounces of jerky

Made with slices of muscle, cut with the grain because we expect our jerky to be a bit chewier than tenderloins, Fajita Jerky is marinated, and then smoked for a unique homemade flavor.

## Ingredients
2 pounds venison
1/3 cup sugar
2 tablespoons salt
1 cup dry red wine
1 medium yellow onion, quartered
4 cloves garlic, minced
1 whole canned jalapeno pepper
1/2 teaspoon cinnamon
1/4 teaspoon dried leaf oregano
1/8 teaspoon ground cloves
1/4 cup sour cream
3 cups mesquite chips

## Preparation
1. Trim the meat, then slice it 1/4 to 1/8 inch thick with the grain. (It's much easier to slice thin when the meat is about half frozen.) Place the sliced meat in a resealable plastic bag.
2. In a blender, puree the sugar, salt, wine, onion, garlic, jalapeno pepper, cinnamon, oregano, cloves and sour cream together. Add to the bag, seal and shake to coat the meat thoroughly. Refrigerate overnight.

## Cooking
1. Remove the meat from the marinade without rinsing and allow it to air dry for an hour. (Lay it on spare cooking grids from the smoker--propped up to circulate air underneath.)
2. Soak the mesquite chips in water 30 minutes before using. Preheat the smoker.
3. Place the meat in the smoker, using 1 cup of mesquite chips for each of the first three hours of smoking. Leave the smoker alone for another 8 hours. When done, the jerky will be dry to the touch but still pliable, not brittle.
4. Place the jerky in a jelly bag and hang for 48 hours to get the surface moisture off. Then store in resealable plastic bags in the refrigerator.

# Trickery Hickory Jerky
Makes 3 ounces of jerky

It tastes like you smoked it, but you didn't. That's the only thing that's 'trickery' in this great jerky recipe.

## Ingredients
1 pound trimmed venison, frozen
1/2 cup Worcestershire sauce
1/2 cup soy sauce
1/2 cup V-8 juice
1/4 cup brown sugar
1/2 teaspoon concentrated liquid hickory smoke
1/2 teaspoon onion powder
1/4 teaspoon garlic powder
1/4 teaspoon black pepper

## Cooking
1. Remove the steaks or roast from the freezer and defrost very briefly, just enough so they'll be very firm for slicing thin jerky.
2. In a resealable plastic bag, combine the Worcestershire sauce, soy sauce, V-8, brown sugar, liquid smoke, onion powder, garlic powder, and pepper. Stir until the solids have dissolved, then add the thinly sliced steak. Seal the bag and marinate in the refrigerator for one hour only.
3. Drain the marinade off the steak slices and let them sit at room temperature for 15 minutes. Preheat the oven to 200°F.
4. Arrange the jerky on metal grids, and place in the oven. (You may want to put aluminum foil under them to keep the mess to a minimum.)
5. Cook 4-6 hours until all the pink is gone, but the meat still bends. Remove from the oven and let the jerky cool. Then hang in jelly or mesh bags for 48 hours in a cool dry place to let surface moisture evaporate. Store in plastic bags in the refrigerator.

## Tips & tactics: The Best Cuts for Jerking
The easy thing about burger jerky is that you can toss all the little scraps of meat you've cut from the bones into the jerky pile. On a mature buck or doe that can add up to several pounds, and since these trimmings come from tender and tough parts of the deer, grinding it is the great equalizer.

Cut-meat jerky requires slightly more thought. Shoulder meat is a good choice since it tends to be tougher than the hind quarter meat. But any meat that's not tender enough for steaks and not too sinewy to cause chewing problems later, is a good candidate. It all depends on how much you like jerky and how tough or tender each individual animal is. I know one case of a tenderloin being better as jerky than almost anything else. The animal was an old trophy mountain goat, and the hunter had three teenage boys to feed.

The other thing to remember whenever you're slicing meat this thin is that larger chunks of meat fare better in the freezer, longer, than smaller ones. Larger chunks have less exterior surface area per pound of meat than smaller chunks, and ground meat and thin jerky slices have the worst surface area to pound ratio of all. The point is don't slice up all your jerky at once. Estimate how much jerky you'll eat in 3-4 months then make up only that much at a time. Once jerked, bag and refrigerate what you'll eat in 2-3 weeks, then vacuum seal or tightly double wrap the rest and freeze it.

# Zesty Old World Jerky
Makes 6 ounces jerky

Multiply the recipe as needed--but only up to four times, max-- for however much meat you want to jerk. Cake cooling racks or jerky making metal grids make good vehicles for moving jerky in and out of the oven, and for cooling it when done. The trouble with cake cooling racks, however, is that they aren't make for being *in* the oven and often one or two solder-joints pop. They do however come footed, so you don't have to prop up the trays for drying and cooling on the counter. (The jerky racks I've seen don't have that feature.) So go buy 2 or 3 cake cooling racks strictly for jerky making; thee's no sense in making the cookie baker unhappy.

## Ingredients
2 tablespoons brown sugar
1 tablespoon salt
1 tablespoon paprika
1/4 teaspoon white pepper
1/4 teaspoon black pepper
1/2 teaspoon dry Coleman's mustard
1 tablespoon dried onion flakes
2 pounds venison roast

## Cooking
1. Combine the spices and pour into a shaker jar. (Old spice jars with large holes work best.) Trim the meat, then slice it 1/4 to 1/8 inch thick with the grain. (It's much easier to slice evenly when the meat is about 98% frozen. For a 2 pound roast like this, I'll thaw 1 minute on the microwave's defrost cycle. That 1/8-inch or less of thawed meat gives the knife a good toe hold, and keeps it from bouncing off.)
2. Preheat the oven to 180°F. Sprinkle some of the spice mix on a cutting board or large platter; lay the sliced meat in a single layer on it. Sprinkle the top of the meat, too. Repeat as needed, transferring the seasoned meat to metal grids as you work.
3. Arrange the jerky on metal grids, and place in the oven. (You may want to put aluminum foil under them to keep the mess to a minimum.)
4. Cook about 4 to 6 hours or until all the pink is gone but the meat still bends, then remove from the oven and let it cool completely at room temperature. Hang in jelly or mesh bags for 48 hours in a cool dry place to allow surface moisture to evaporate, then store in plastic bags in the refrigerator; for longer than 2-3 weeks storage, vacuum seal and freeze.

# Mexican Mole Jerky
Makes 6 ounces of jerky

Another cut-meat jerky, the mole sports the chocolate undertones of the classic Mexican mole sauce (pronounced MOE-lay) and a multitude of other spices. This is a nuanced flavor, rather than the simple lots-o-salt and oh-my-gosh-pepper flavor that characterizes a lot of commercial jerky. I like 3 tablespoons of this seasoning mix per pound of meat; for more intense flavor, use 4 tablespoons per pound. And multiply the recipe up to five times for larger batches. More than that should be a new, different batch of meat and spices to keep the ratios correct.

## Ingredients
1 1/2 teaspoons salt
3/4 teaspoon coarse black pepper
1 tablespoon plus 1 teaspoon white sugar
1 tablespoon dried onion flakes
1/4 teaspoon garlic powder
1 1/2 teaspoons ground cumin
1/2 teaspoon dried red pepper flakes
1/2 teaspoon Hershey's unsweetened (dry) cocoa
1/2 teaspoon sweet paprika
1/8 teaspoon cayenne pepper
2 pound roast, frozen

## Cooking
1. Combine the spices and pour into a shaker jar. (Old spice jars with large holes work best.) Trim the meat, then slice it 1/4 to 1/8 inch thick with the grain. (It's much easier to slice evenly when the meat is about 98% frozen. For a 2 pound roast like this, I'll thaw 1 minute on the microwave's defrost cycle. That 1/8" or less of thawed meat gives the knife a good toe hold, and keeps it from bouncing off.)
2. Preheat the oven to 180°F. Sprinkle some of the spice mix on a cutting board or large platter; lay the sliced meat in a single layer on it. Sprinkle the top of the meat, too. Repeat as needed, transferring the seasoned meat to the metal grids as you work.
3. Arrange the jerky on metal grids, and place in the oven. (You may want to put aluminum foil under them to keep the mess to a minimum.)
4. Cook about 4 hours until all the pink is gone, but the meat still bends, then remove from the oven and let it cool completely. Store in plastic bags in the refrigerator; for longer than 2-3 weeks storage, vacuum seal and freeze.

****This Mole Jerky seasoning mix will also perk up your soups. Try it in your old standby meat and potato stew or in my Boone's Stew: replace the Worcestershire, garlic, and Montreal Steak Seasoning with 1 teaspoon of Mole Jerky mix and a pinch or two of red pepper flakes.

# Pepper Sticks

Makes about 4 ounces of pepper sticks

The fastest way to make sticks is to use a stick attachment on a Jerky Gun, using a ground venison mix. Another way is to spread your mix out on a cookie sheet between two sheets of waxed paper. Then freeze it. Once frozen, turn the frozen mix out on a cutting board and cut 1/2 inch wide strips. Either way will get you perfect pepper sticks.

## Ingredients
1 pound ground venison
1 teaspoon salt
1/2 teaspoon black pepper
1/2 teaspoon garlic powder
1/2 teaspoon onion powder
1/2 teaspoon crushed red pepper flakes

## Cooking
1. Combine all the ingredients in a large bowl, and shape into pepper sticks with a jerky gun, or spread on a cookie sheet between two pieces of waxed paper about 1/4-inch thick, freeze, and then cut. Arrange on mesh metal trays.
2. Heat your oven to 160°F, and cook the pepper sticks until they are not pink inside, but are still moist enough to bend; 4-6 hours for the frozen variety; 2 hours for sticks formed with a jerky gun.
3. Take the jerky out of the oven, still on the mesh cooking trays, and let it cool and dry out for several hours on the counter. Once dried, put the sticks in a jelly or mesh bag and hang for 48 hours in a cool dry place to allow the surface moisture to evaporate. Then store the sticks in resealable plastic bags in the refrigerator, or freezer--if you're planning to store them for more than a couple of weeks.

# Biltong-Style Jerky

Makes 4 ounces of biltong

Biltong is the African version of jerky, and this is John's favorite, because there is very little flavoring: the meat is what he wants to taste.

## Ingredients
1 pound ground venison
4 teaspoons Worcestershire sauce
3/4 teaspoon salt
3/4 teaspoon pepper

## Cooking
1. Combine all the ingredients in a large bowl, and shape into jerky strips (about 1" wide, 1/4" thick) with a jerky gun. If you don't own a jerky gun, line a cookie sheet with waxed paper, spread the burger mixture out, and press flat, about 1/4" thick. (Use a rolling pin or empty wine bottle to even up the thickness.) Cover with waxed paper.
2. Freeze overnight; then pop the frozen slab onto a cutting board and cut as above for strips. Place on a tight-mesh cooking rack.
3. Heat your oven to 160°F, and cook the biltong until it's not pink inside, about 4 hours for frozen burger, 2 for jerky gun burger.
4. Take the biltong out of the oven, still on the mesh cooking trays, and let it cool and dry out for several hours on the counter. Once dried, transfer to a jelly or mesh bag and let it hang for 48 hours in a cool dry place to let the surface moisture evaporate. Store the biltong in resealable plastic bags in the refrigerator up to 2 weeks. If you're planning to store them for more than a couple of weeks, keep them in the freezer.

## Tips & Tactics: When Is It done?

A lot of old jerky recipes call for cooking 1/4" thick slices at 160°F for 11 hours. In my oven, cooking these recipes at 180° for more than 7 hours risks charring them. It always dries them out too much. Just look at commercial jerky: it's pliable, meat-colored, and a tad juicy--not crisp, black, and dry as dust. True, commercial jerky is made with preservatives, but they're also stored at room temperature in the store. For that convenience, we get to eat nitrates.

The advantage of homemade jerky is no nitrates, but you don't have to char it to make it safe to eat. I figure that's why refrigerators and freezers were invented. Plus, I went to high school: I know how to count up to 14 days and only leave my jerky refrigerated that long. The rest is frozen. Nuff said.

So, if we don't char the jerky, how DO we know when the it's done? Like all long, slow cooking, there's no pink in the middle. And since jerky is cooked at such a low temperature, you have some fudge room: is the pink all gone? If not, cook it another 30 minutes. But the jerky should also still bend a bit, though not sag when held by one end. Right from the oven jerky still has some moisture, so let it cool and air, propped on the cooling racks for a few hours before bagging it up. If you have the room and time, hang it in cotton jelly bags in a cool dry place for another 48 hours, and that will take care of any residual moisture.

Having said that, I need to tell you Montana is an ideal climate for drying things out. There are times when relative humidity falls into the teens. (High summer, and high furnace season come to mind.) So finding a dry place to hang jelly bags is easy for me. For moister climes, like Alabama or Pennsylvania choose your days. Don't jerk in the rain or in high humidity. Or, skip this step, you'll only add moisture. Get the pink out, cool on the counter, then refrigerate or freeze.

# Summer Jerky
Makes 4 ounces of jerky

This one uses Morton's Tender Quick which will give you that nice red color of commercially prepared jerky. It's the nitrates that do it. But as you'll note, since there's salt in the TQ, there is no other salt in the recipe. The only trick to adding nitrates is to do it 24 hours before you start cooking the jerky. Adding the spices then, too, just saves time. And if you find you prefer the unique flavor nitrates add, you can use TQ in the other jerky recipes in this book by just substituting it for the salt already in the recipe. (1 tablespoon per pound of meat) I have to admit that in corned meat, I prefer the nitrate version. It's a matter of taste.

## Ingredients
1 tablespoon Morton's Tender Quick
1/4 teaspoon chili powder
1/8 teaspoon dry mustard
1 pound ground venison

## Cooking
1. Sprinkle the Tender Quick, chili powder, and dry mustard over the meat and mix thoroughly by hand. Cover and let the cure and the spices work 24 hours in the refrigerator.
2. Shape your jerky into sticks with a jerky gun, or spread the jerky mix onto a cookie sheet, between two pieces of waxed paper, about 1/4 inch thick and freeze. Once frozen, pop the jerky mix out on a cutting board, and cut 1-inch wide strips, 4 to 6 inches long.
3. Transfer to a metal mesh grid, and place in a 160°F oven. Let it cook 2 hours if you used a jerky gun, 4 hours if you used the freezing method.
4. Take the jerky out of the oven, still on the grids, and let it cool and dry out for several hours on the counter. Once dried, transfer to a jelly or mesh bag and let it hang for 48 hours in a cool dry place to let the surface moisture evaporate. Store the sticks in resealable plastic bags in the refrigerator—or freezer, if you're planning to store them for more than a couple of weeks.

# Why This Book?

This is Eileen's eighth cookbook, the second one exclusively about big game. Why would anyone need to write so much about big game cooking? It may have something to do with the three freezers in the basement, and the fact that she and her husband John Barsness eat game at least 350 days a year. (You've got to eat a donut once in a while.)

Eileen has also been a game cooking columnist for two national magazines, but this book marks a departure from both columns and previous cookbooks: she's self publishing it. Why? Because this is the book she's proposed several times over the years and no one has thought it commercial enough. It's about butchering big game animals for your family, and offering variations on the basic butchering cuts so what you cut fits your family even though each family is different, and changes over the years as well. It's also the first of her books to include side dishes--something her fans have been asking for for years. (As in, "Okay here's the moose steak, but what the devil do I serve with it?")

Well, here are the moose, antelope, elk, deer, and caribou steak, along with hints on how to judge and cook them and the exotic animals (and native bison) we're all testing our rifles on, plus the side dishes that go with them. Nothing fancy, just lots of good meat and potatoes, with a side of marinade. Lots of marinades, because if you eat a lot of game and hunt a lot of game, you're going to need a little help in the kitchen to provide a bit more variety in your diet. (Then there's the once-in-a-lifetime, just at the wrong-end-of-the-season set of antlers that walks into your crosshairs. And as you pull the trigger, you're thinking, that's gonna need some help. From forkhorns to big bulls, that's what this book is about.)

There are lots of how-to pictures, the latest scientific research on meat care, and a couple of time and temperature tables that make roasting rumps and tenderloins as easy as grilling steaks. Recipes galore. And then there's the family photo album. A Rogues' Gallery of more than 60 years combined, the best and worst animals John and Eileen have tipped over, cut up, and cooked. How real animals, real weather, and stupid animal behavior--using the best game care methods they know--ended up tasting and chewing at the table.

What John and Eileen have found in their travels is that we are not alone. Hunters all over the world want the same things: tender and mild tasting game. The best way to put that lovely morsel on your fork is to cut it up yourself. John and Eileen have been killing and cutting their own for a long, long time. And fooling lots of people into enjoying their least favorite game. Buy this book and never pay a processor again.